AF392577

ESCAPE FROM JAVA

Escape from Java

By Cornelis van der Grift
and E. H. Lansing

THOMAS Y. CROWELL COMPANY

NEW YORK

1943

COPYRIGHT 1943
BY CORNELIS VAN DER GRIFT

All rights reserved. No part of this book may be reproduced in any form except by a reviewer who may quote brief passages in a review to be printed in a magazine or newspaper

THIS IS A WARTIME BOOK PRODUCED IN FULL COMPLIANCE WITH GOVERNMENT REGULATIONS FOR CONSERVATION OF PAPER AND OTHER ESSENTIAL MATERIALS.

AN UNCOMMON VALOR REPRINT EDITION
Complete and Unabridged

Printed in the United States of America

ISBN: 979-8-8690-9410-0

CHAPTER ONE

"De Japanners zullen Java nooit krijgen."

That's what they said in Batavia. "The Japs will never get Java." It wasn't only the Batavians who felt this way. People all over the island believed it. I suppose it was natural. No one thinks it can happen to him.

You can't blame them for believing as they did. When you have lived in a place for hundreds of years and built it into one of the wealthiest and best-governed islands in the world, it's difficult to imagine that anyone can take it away from you. Java is a beautiful spot, lying, as someone has said, "like a belt of emeralds around the equator." Its abundant foliage seems to burst from the ground; flowers, trees, and shrubs are everywhere. Most of the white population lived on the plantations in the interior or in the large cities. Batavia, with its attractive streets, large squares, the clubs, the great hotels like the Hotel des Indes, said to be the best hotel in the Far East, was a city of extraordinary charm.

Java was my home for twenty-two years. I came to the island from Holland when I was a child of six. Except for two years at a university "at home" and occasional short visits to other countries, I was in Java continuously. But living on an island did not give me an insular point of view. I have always been interested in outside events, have tried to interpret them and their effect on the world as a whole.

It should be understood that it was the white population,

[1

together with the large group of Indonesian intellectuals, who had the greatest interest in world affairs. The Indonesian peasant lives more isolated from the rest of mankind. These Javanese farmers are gentle people. They live a peaceful life in their inland villages, high on the slopes of the great volcanic mountains or in the valleys between. The cultivation of their rice crops, the communal village life, their families and their simple amusements occupy their attention primarily. Even those who live in cities like Batavia or Surabaya have not become sophisticated in any sense of the word.

There are forty-seven million Indonesians like this on the island of Java as compared to two hundred thousand Europeans, chiefly Dutch; six hundred thousand Chinese and an insignificant sprinkling of four or five thousand Japanese.

I have no intention of trying to make this book a comprehensive history of Java, its people, their customs, habits, and general way of life. Anyone can find these facts in countless books, all of which are far more detailed and learned than anything I care to attempt. This is the story of what I personally know about Java, how the threat of Japanese conquest affected me, how I lived under the so-called Jap "co-prosperity" rule and finally how I escaped from it. But in order to give some idea of Java, the governmental center of the East Indies, a brief sketch of its history and its people may not be out of place.

Except for a brief period in the early nineteenth century, Holland has controlled the East Indies since the beginning of the seventeenth century. It is no use pretending that the Dutch overlordship has always been a model of orderliness and benevolence. In the early years some of the Dutch governors, like the administrators of other European-ruled colonies, were harsh and overbearing to an extreme. But for the last hundred years, the Dutch administration has been a just and understanding rule that has made the Netherlands East Indies one of the happiest and most prosperous areas in the world.

One of the principles of the Dutch government has been to respect Indonesian culture and to develop it along their own lines. The Javanese culture is an ancient one and any attempt to force the Indonesians into the ways of so-called civilization would be not only difficult but criminally stupid. The Dutch have always been careful to preserve *adat*, or the native law, and the Indonesians appreciate this respect for their age-old manners and customs.

As an instance it can be mentioned that the government built modern irrigation systems for the native *sawahs*, or rice fields, a vast improvement over the crude mud walls and dams of former times, which crumbled away during each rainy season. The peasants liked the new system, but no amount of persuasion could make them use a sickle instead of a hand knife to gather the crop. "The grain would be offended if we used such rude methods," was their explanation. And so the rice is gently cut a few stalks at a time on the theory that it will be better pleased by such thoughtful treatment.

Each village—and there are many of them on the thickly populated island of Java, where 821 people live crowded within each of its fifty-one thousand square miles—has its own administration. The village chief is the man to whom the Javanese look for a solution to all their problems and disputes. Though the government is naturally a court of last appeal in case of necessity, it in reality interferes as little as possible in local matters. A European is not allowed to buy land from the natives, for the rice fields are handed down from father to son among the natives and the Dutch have no desire to upset this natural order of succession.

Of course, there is a large group of intellectual Javanese and these people take great interest in administrative and cultural affairs. The People's Council in Java is composed of sixty men; thirty of them Javanese, five Orientals, and twenty-five Dutch. This Council, with its predominating native influence, is the real law-making body in Java.

From my own intimate knowledge of the Javanese I can state as a fact that the natives are not in any sense oppressed by the Dutch living on their island. Among the intellectuals there is a group that works toward self-government for Java, but the Dutch do not suppress it; in fact, they are encouraging an educational program that will allow the Javanese a larger share in the administration. The Indonesians as a whole appreciate the advantages that the white people have given them; the tremendous improvements in sanitation, the modern schools which anyone is free to attend, and, above all, the wisdom the Dutch have shown in allowing them to lead their own lives and pursue their own interests.

The Chinese in Java have fitted themselves into the island life so well that they are a welcome and necessary part of it. Generally speaking, the Chinese are the shopkeepers. They operate good stores and give liberal credit to the natives; something which is highly appreciated, though it sometimes leads to usury. The fact that the Chinese show a profit under this system at the end of a business year is a major miracle. But they flourish under it and many of them are third and fourth generation Chinese. In every sense of the word they are loyal and essential citizens of the country.

But long before the shadows of war began to fall on the Indies, the scant Japanese population in Java was an "outside element" in the peaceful island life. Though the four or five thousand Japs among the teeming millions in Java were scarcely noticeable, they succeeded in making themselves felt. Perhaps their pushing ambition, their determination to "get ahead," were not understood in Java. A native Javanese is happy as long as he has a belly full of rice. A Jap wants something more. In Java, as we were soon to discover, he wanted complete pictures of the military and naval fortifications, of the roads, railways, and harbor works. The barbers, hairdressers, and, above all, the photographers who carried on their business in Batavia and elsewhere saw that the Son of Heaven got these pictures. The photographers in particular were in an ideal position to get what they wanted from Java. A major in the Japanese Army worked for several years as a photographer on one of the main streets of Batavia. He is probably a general now.

The influence of Japan itself was not considerable in Java. By 1939 the Japanese exports to the Netherlands Indies were but fourteen per cent of the total imports of the Indies, while our exports were considerably less. It was in the fall of 1940 that representatives of the Empire of the Rising Sun came to Batavia to suggest to the Dutch government that Japan would be only too willing to help share the white man's burden in Java. After allowing the representatives to cool their heels for several months, the Dutch officials politely told them that they could get along very well without Japanese "co-prosperity." They were committed to the development of the country on behalf of the Indonesians and couldn't take on any further obligations. The Japanese trade commission returned home in the middle of 1941 with much loss of face and a rankling grievance against the Dutch.

But this visit of the Japanese economic experts was not the first intimation that the Netherlands government received that the island empire to the north was in danger of becoming a yellow peril. As early as 1930 the Dutch knew that the Japs were building up a strong military machine and that they had no intentions of using it merely for show purposes. Though this was long before the "incident" in Manchukuo and an enemy invasion of Java seemed as remote as a threat from Mars, plans were made to blow up the oil fields and other industrial developments in Java and to destroy the tin-mining islands, such as Bangka and Billiton, in case of attack.

Plans like this were necessary in view of the military situation in the Indies. The East Indies are spread over an area as large as the United States and they consist of countless islands, some of which are in a relatively primitive condition, many of them sparsely settled and all so widely scattered that a military defense system for the entire group is an impossibility. Therefore, it was principally Java, the seat-of government and the most important island, that the Dutch hoped to defend from aggression.

Ten years ago, when I was eighteen, I took my year's military service, as all Europeans in the Indies are required to do. Every four years a compulsory refresher course was given, so that the white population as a whole knew what army life was. It wasn't until 1941 that the Indonesians were conscripted, though many of them served voluntarily in the militia.

By the end of 1941 there were about a hundred thousand men in the army, some Dutch but most of them native. This was a relatively small number to defend an island like Java with its exposed coastline and few natural defenses. But we couldn't get the matériel to equip more. The navy was no better off. It consisted of five cruisers, twenty submarines, six or eight destroyers, and a few torpedo boats with auxiliaries. The naval base at Surabaya on the eastern end of the island is a naturally fine harbor, large enough to base a navy twenty times the size of ours. But those few ships were all we had. The air force was more promising. We had at the end of 1941 four hundred fighter planes and bombers, most of which, however, were not the latest type and were inferior to the Japanese Zero.

The weakness of our Army, Navy, and Air Force was no fault of the Netherlands Indies government. The Indies have no heavy industries and they are consequently dependent upon the industrialized countries for tanks, guns, planes, and other war matériel. Even before the fall of Holland in May, 1940, the army and navy men in Java had been working to build up their strength. Large orders were placed, but in the general race for armament only a small part came to the Indies. We were insufficiently geared for modern warfare.

CHAPTER TWO

THE Jap attack on Pearl Harbor set in train a course of events that is all too horribly familiar to everyone. We in Java had to watch the tide of conquest creep closer and closer, while we did everything in our power to prepare for any eventuality. And though some of us knew that a real defense of the island was impossible, since we just didn't have the war matériel, there was never a moment of despair.

The first thing the government did, naturally, was to intern all the Japs on the islands. But long ago they had finished their work there and Java was an open book to the war lords of Tokyo, just as Singapore and Pearl Harbor were. Of course the Netherlands government declared war on Japan immediately, and a large part of the 250,000 to 300,000 Dutch and Europeans on the islands were called into the army. Precautions were taken to guard Batavia, and the building of air-raid shelters, already begun with the fall of Holland, was speeded up. Everyone on Java had some part in its defense; working at civil-defense jobs, if they weren't in the army.

Major General Hein ter Poorten, chief of staff of the Netherlands East Indian Army, was as ready as any man could be with the material he had to work with. Ter Poorten is a realist. He always knew the Japs had big ideas and he'd done all in his power to build up and modernize the army.

For years he'd worked to increase the air force, too, and what success our planes had against the enemy in the early months of the war was largely due to his foresight in training pilots and ground crews. Major General van Oyen, chief of the air force, was also alive to the dangers of our position. He worked closely with ter Poorten and helped in the establishment of the airdromes scattered throughout the interior of the island. I often think what these two men must have felt as they watched the Japs roll nearer and nearer, knowing as they did what matériel they had to fight them off.

There were a few munitions factories in Java and they had turned out a good many bullets, bombs, shells, grenades, and torpedoes. But after the war in Europe started, it was almost impossible to get any more raw materials and, as I've already said, we had no luck getting sufficient finished stuff from England or America.

It's Admiral Helfrich that most people outside of Java remember as the hero of our short-lived fight against the Japs. In the first fifty-four days of the war, his ships sank fifty-four enemy ships. We called him Ship-a-day Helfrich. The Admiral is also a realist. He knew what he had to fight with and against what. But that knowledge never led him to try to conserve our meager fleet when there was the slightest chance of doing damage with it. Time after time in those early days of the war he would send out a mere handful of ships against the fleets of transports and convoys that flowed south from Japan. One of our subs sank four Jap transports the day after Pearl Harbor. But the Japs always had more transports and more bandy-legged, bespectacled soldiers to fill them.

Our naval forces in the Indies were part of the Allied Nations plan of defense for the whole Pacific area. The American Admiral Hart was the chief and Admiral Helfrich his second in command. Helfrich had studied plans of naval defense for the islands for years; it was something of a hobby with him. For years he had felt that one day the Japs would attack the Indies.

Again it's too late to talk about what might have been done, but I can't help wondering what might have happened if Helfrich had had his way with sufficient ships and planes. He knows the Indies as well as he knows the palm of his hand. Even by the middle of February, when Hart retired and Helfrich took command, it was not too late. Although several of our ships were gone, taking a lot of Japs with them, the main body of our fleet was still there, assisted by American and British forces. And how they fought and what they could do was demonstrated in the battle in Macassar Strait, the battle of Bali, and finally the battle in the Java Sea.

I remember what it was like to watch the Japs coming nearer and nearer. By the end of January they had taken Manila, Hong Kong, and were creeping southward in Malaya closer and closer to Singapore. They had landed troops in Sarawak and on Celebes. Tarakan, the oil island off the coast of Borneo, had fallen. That's the place where a heavy oil comes from the earth in so pure a state that it can be pumped right from the wells into the tanks of a ship without refining. The island couldn't be defended but our troops had wrecked the oil wells before leaving. It would take at least half a year to get them working again. In every one of the places from which our troops were forced back, they scorched the earth thoroughly before leaving. We left nothing for the Japs except destruction.

In Batavia the general feeling was still one of confidence. Now, however, instead of saying only, "The Japs will never take Java," they said, "We'll defend Java to the last. They will never take Java." They knew now that we would be attacked, but they still couldn't believe we would be conquered. Help was expected from the outside to replace our losses in the defense of Singapore and the outer islands. We didn't let ourselves down. There was still time for replacements to come in.

The Battle of Macassar Strait at the end of January proved this point. Against heavy odds the United Nations planes met a large Jap convoy escorting transports in the narrow passage between Celebes and Borneo, on their way to invade Java. In the ensuing battle thirty-one of the transports were sunk as well as several of the escorting warships. The battle was a tremendous victory for the Allies. Though the Japs landed on Borneo and in a short time took Balikpapan, which couldn't be defended and was completely destroyed, the invasion of Java was prevented and time was gained. The Batavians were enormously cheered by the sinking of the ships in Macassar Strait; and though the oil center of Balikpapan had fallen, they were full of confidence and said, "The Japs will never take Java."

Certainly such confidence was wonderful for the morale of the city and its people. They didn't really need the posters that the government pasted up on the streets. These posters repeated the famous slogan, emanating from the Spanish civil war: "It is better to die on your feet than live on your knees." The Dutch don't need to be told that.

The native population had by this time become fully conscious of the war. When the men in the families were drafted into the army, they naturally knew that their peaceful way of life had changed and that it was due for an even greater upheaval. Stories of what it would be like to live under Japanese rule began to be whispered about. The Indonesians knew that the Japs paid low wages and one of their principal fears was that under Jap law they would get less money. Their fears were justified, as will soon be seen. More important was their feeling for the Dutch. They had been happy under our government, they had been allowed to live their own lives and they didn't want any changes. No Indonesian does; he wants to work the same fields, live in the same bamboo house, sing the same songs, and act in general just as his forebears have for hundreds of years. It didn't look as though the Japs would let them keep their old life.

It wasn't until the first part of February that the war really came to Java, however. Then the Japs started bombing us. After heavy fighting they took the island of Amboina, which lies to the east of Celebes and was our second largest naval base in the Indies. Their bombers appeared over Surabaya and Batavia, not doing a great deal of damage, but "softening" us up, as they thought. Their troops were close behind, creeping southward in Borneo, Celebes, and in Malaya. There was no doubt that Java was their next objective.

Our air force and ships did what they could. Every day we heard that so many Jap planes had been shot down, so many ships sunk. By this time a few American Flying Fortresses had arrived to help us. But they weren't enough. In a way they only served as an aggravation, for we knew what could have been done if we had had more of these amazing bombers. The spirit of our airmen, soldiers, and sailors was wonderful. It never seemed to occur to them that they were waging a losing fight. They went out and did what they had to do; they could sink Jap ships, down dozens of planes, but it was never enough. The Japs always had more.

When Singapore fell on the fifteenth of February we were only partly prepared for it. That is, as prepared as anyone could be for the downfall of what we had always felt to be the strongest fortified position in the world. By that time so much had happened to change our way of thinking that we didn't bother to be surprised at anything. All we knew was that we would be next, unless help came in.

The British troops began to come into Java after Singapore went; those who had succeeded in escaping from Malaya. I won't forget them. Naturally they were disorganized. They had had to flee in any way they could, some coming by boat, some by plane. Lots of them were Anzacs, Australian and New Zealand men. They had been through hell on Malaya and they'd lost the fight. That's enough to take it out of a soldier. I remember talking to a New Zealander in a bar in Batavia. He'd just landed that morning from a native fishing boat, or *prahu* as they are called in the Indies. He'd lost all his equipment, his rifle, ammunition and all his belongings. But he didn't care about that. All he wanted to do was get down to Chilachap on the south coast of Java where some British boats were picking up their troops and taking them back to Australia.

"Just let me at those — — —" he kept saying. "God, if we'd had the stuff, we'd have — — — those Japs."

You couldn't write what he said, but I knew what he meant. He wanted to fight Japs. There were a lot of British troops in Java then and they all wanted to get out so they could carry on the fight somewhere else. They knew Java was gone already. They'd seen what kind of stuff the Japs had to fight with and they knew we had nothing to compare with it.

But even after Singapore fell, the people in Java did not despair. I don't suppose anyone had much doubt about what was going to happen to us, but you'd never have known it from a Dutchman in Batavia. I had dinner at the Hotel des Indes one evening shortly after we heard the news about Singapore. Only a few people were having cocktails on the terrace, served by the native waiters with their usual polite efficiency. The talk was different. It was about war. But the women were as beautifully dressed as ever, the men looked cool and comfortable in their linen dinner jackets. There is an almost indescribable sense of ease about the hotel and one felt it, even with the Jap at the door, so to speak. However, the fact that one could have dinner at the hotel, just as one always had during the long years of peace, shouldn't give anyone the impression that the Dutch were "fiddling while Rome burned." They just refused to let themselves show what they felt. We had done everything in our power to prepare for the defense of the island. The Dutch were having a last drink to wish us all luck.

It was the fall of Palembang, the rich oil city in Sumatra, that hit us even harder than Singapore's collapse. This happened not many days after we heard the news of Singapore. The refugees from Palembang came crowding into Batavia on ferries, fishing boats, anything they could find. They told stories of the Jap conquest of the city that gave us an ugly premonition of what we were to face. The Dutch had blown up the huge oil wells immediately and the roaring fires from these wells and refineries impressed the people even more than the actual Jap attack. The sound of the flames and the heavy clouds of smoke were a terrifying experience. Over and over again I heard people tell what they had felt when they saw these millions of dollars worth of installations going up in smoke.

These refugees brought with them some of the script that the Japs had prepared for the countries they conquered. There were banknotes corresponding to our five and one guilder notes and even for one-cent notes. The Japs forced this script on the people of the conquered countries in exchange for real currency. It wasn't worth the paper it was printed on, but the Japs used it to help along their "co-prosperity." It doesn't need much insight to see who prospered by this exchange of banknotes.

The refugees also told of the Jap paratroops who had been principally responsible for taking Palembang. They were heavily armed when they landed from the sky, and the Dutch and Indonesian troops who were there to meet them were pitifully outnumbered. But our men charged into the Japs, armed only with bayonets. Of course, against such a well-equipped enemy they could do nothing, but they weren't going to let that stop them from trying. They fought themselves to death, and thus gained time for the destruction squads to do their work. Palembang fell but the riches of southern Sumatra were demolished. No oil for the Japs.

CHAPTER THREE

THE Japs were closing the jaws of a trap about us. They had control of Sumatra to the west and now they began bombing Timor and Bali to the east. Our planes and ships, with the aid of the British and American units that had been sent to hold Java, went out to meet the swarming, always more numerous Jap ships and planes. On Timor and Bali our land army fought fiercely. But we hadn't enough men or machines to meet the attack. The Japs landed at Timor and Bali, taking their losses as part of the price of eventual victory. They secured their positions around Java, tightening their jaws to swallow us.

Finally Australian and American troops landed on Java. Their presence was heartening and disheartening at the same time. If our Allies were landing troops, they must feel there was hope for the island, but we saw how few of them came. The natives' morale rose with a bound at the sight of the Americans. These easy, confident men looked enormous to the small-sized Indonesians. "Long live America," they shouted, whenever they saw an American soldier. "You will beat the dwarfs!" An American looked a match for a dozen tiny Japs. But there were too many dwarfs, even for the Americans—too many and too well equipped.

It was the Battle of the Java Sea, immediately following the Jap landings at Timor and Bali, that decided the fate of Java. A tremendous Jap convoy was sighted in the waters between Borneo and Java. It was headed in our direction. Our last chance had come to ward off the fate which hung over us. Outnumbered, outgunned, Admiral Helfrich sent the last of his ships to meet the attack. He must have known that the battle was lost, even before it began, but, if the Japs were going to take Java, they were going to pay for it; and the price for this richest isle of the Indies was high. Five Jap cruisers, three destroyers, and seventeen transports were sunk or crippled by our ships.

We started the war with five cruisers. Two were lost in the Battle of the Java Sea, as well as an undisclosed number of destroyers and lighter naval units. Though we sank more ships than the Japs, the contest was unequal. They always had more; we had lost the strength of our fleet. Our last naval base in the Indies was threatened. To all intents the battle for Java was lost when the score was reckoned after that heroic sea engagement. Now Java lay open to the invaders, for with the loss of our planes in the defense of Malaya and the islands outside Java, our land forces were easy prey for the Japanese bombers and fighters.

The Japs wasted no time. It was too late for the few hundred planes that might have saved us; for the necessary troops to bolster our army, aided by the few thousand Allied soldiers. The Jap plan of attack was obvious. We knew where they'd strike and we'd made what preparations we could to meet them. The north coast of Java is flat, broad and open.

There are no natural defenses there, no hope of guarding it with the forces at our command. Our main bastion was at Bandung, where General Headquarters had been established within the encircling hills of this inland city on the west.

All roads leading to Bandung were mined, every mountain pass was planted with explosives. It was here that we were to make our last stand for Java.

The Japs landed from barges at four points on the island; at the east and west and at Indramayu and Rembang on the north coast. They made for the airdromes in the interior. Those that came from Indramayu were headed for Kalijati, the big airport at the foot of the mountains surrounding Bandung. In the east they immobilized the area around Surabaya, our naval base. They came inland from Indramayu and cut the railroad between Batavia and Surabaya. The forces from Rembang headed for the oilfields at Tjepu, which the Dutch destroyed before they left. With rapid, slashing strokes they cut up the northern coast and flanked Batavia and Surabaya. They pushed on toward Bandung. Within two days they were thirty miles from the mountain fortress.

The conquest of Java wasn't easy for the Japs. Though our troops were pitifully undersupplied with artillery and had insufficient mechanized equipment, they fought wherever they could hit a Jap and gave the enemy a harrowing few days. Bridges, roads, and airdromes were wrecked before the Japs came. Everything of military value was destroyed by the retreating forces, who left nothing but ruin behind them. We slowed the Japs, but could not stop them. Our planes had fought well while they lasted, but, once a plane was shot down, there wasn't another to take its place to defend Java. The Jap troops came nearer to Bandung along the mined roads, across the devastated areas the Dutch had left in their wake.

There was no chance for guerrilla warfare on the plains

of Java. It is too densely populated, too thickly overlaid with roads and railways. With 821 people living within each square mile a guerrilla has nowhere to hide. Much of the island is flat, open country, in spite of the volcanic mountains in the interior. We had no choice but to stick to the one feasible plan of defense; to make a stand at Bandung.

At Batavia we knew the end was near. Rumors spread that a huge force of American troops was on its way to help us; that an Allied fleet was even now preparing to attack the Jap transports which brought the invaders to Java. Though we listened to these stories, we knew them to be false. Then, five days after the initial Jap landings, Batavia had to be evacuated by the army, as the railway to Bandung was threatened. Before leaving, the army destroyed everything in the city that might be of value to the Japs: the major government buildings, the harbor works at Tanjung Priok, all the oil-storage tanks and other industrial works. All private cars were commandeered to get the soldiers to Bandung, where they were to join in the defense of that stronghold. Those cars which the army could not use were dismantled. Only a few government automobiles were left on the streets.

Thus when the Japs came to Batavia, the entire population was there to face them. No private citizen had been able to leave the city, for there was no transportation. Indonesians and Europeans alike were on hand to take whatever treatment the invaders chose to give them. Batavia fell on March 5, 1942. At seven-thirty that evening the Resident sent volunteers out with white flags to receive the commander of the enemy forces, west of the city.

I was a civilian member of the Netherlands Army, delegated to carry on my work in Batavia. My job was in the office of one of the public utilities, a position I had held for several years. Just a few days before the occupation those who did essential work were instructed by the Dutch government to stick by their jobs. The only precaution we took for our personal safety was to destroy our uniforms. We'd get a better chance with the Japs if they thought we were civilians. So I had a front-row seat for the tragedy which followed.

Though I had seen nothing of the actual battle for Java and, except for the ineffectual and occasional bombing of the city, had experienced none of its reality, I was not unprepared for the announcement that Batavia was to be surrendered. The news we had received in the past weeks was all too significant to anyone who could read the story of Jap conquest in recent months. Therefore, the government radio announcement which came a few hours before the capitulation, telling of the imminent surrender of the city, was not surprising. But it was a shock nonetheless. Right up to the last we had been hoping for some miracle to save us. That miracle never happened. Like the Philippines, Malaya, and the other Pacific islands, we had fallen victim to the tide of conquest. Java was lost.

The government broadcast a warning that all civilians stay off the streets that night of March fifth. The officials wanted no "incidents" to give the Japs an excuse to terrorize the population. But, like many Batavians both white and native, I could not resist the impulse to see what was happening. It wasn't a spectacle that anyone wanted to watch, but, like torturing an aching tooth, you couldn't help it. A crowd gathered in front of the Residental Building, where we knew the formal surrender of the city was to take place.

The volunteers who had gone out to meet the officers of the Jap forces brought them into the city in the early evening. The native and Dutch policemen, who were on hand to keep the gathering crowd orderly, cleared a path for the general's car through the throng. No one spoke. We moved back when the police asked us to, but we did so quietly. It was amid a grim, disheartened silence that the Jap officers walked up the steps to the Resident's office and took possession of the city.

A contingent of Jap troops followed immediately on bicycles; small, low machines especially built to accommodate the bandy-legged warriors. It was too dark to see much. I couldn't even make out what the Jap soldiers looked like, except that they were little men, heavily armed and extremely businesslike. Later I learned that there were about two thousand of them in this advance guard.

The troops took over the duty of policing the crowd. Armed with rifles and machine guns they threw a ring around the building and began eyeing the throng with obvious suspicion. They knew that the Dutch government had asked people to stay at home and this gathering looked like insubordination to them.

The onlookers began to get restless. They had expected a show of some sort and nothing was happening. Some people began pushing their way through the police lines toward the building. The Jap guards got nervous. They tried to push the curious natives, who made up the greater part of the throng, back with the flat of their swords. But the Indonesians were persistent. Without a second's hesitation, the Japs turned their machine guns on them and fired.

Several natives and one or two Dutch policemen were killed. A man who had been standing near me fell to his knees, his chest torn by a spray of bullets. The crowd lost its curiosity to know what the Japs were like. Silently the people disbanded, taking their dead and wounded with them. We had had our first taste of Jap "co-prosperity."

CHAPTER FOUR

IT wasn't until the next morning that I had a good look at the Jap occupation troops. By the time I was ready to go to work, as I had been instructed, the Jap soldiers were all over the city. They came by bicycle. Swarms of squat little men on their strange machines. They came waving tiny Japanese flags, showing their buck teeth in wide grins and feeling very happy. Their black eyes glinted behind their horn-rimmed spectacles. Within half an hour I was able to estimate that fifty per cent of the Japs wore glasses.

The ordinary Jap soldier is not a prepossessing specimen of the human race. Most of them are bowlegged, with stunted, awkward bodies and extremely ugly faces. The caricatures one sees of the Japs aren't much exaggerated. They look that way: runty, bespectacled, and big toothed. Many of them drag their feet when they walk, scuffing along as though it were too much of an effort to lift them off the ground.

I was surprised at their lack of equipment. From the glimpse I had had of the invaders the night before, I supposed that every soldier would be heavily armed. But most of the men I saw this morning carried only small-bore rifles. About one in twenty-five had a machine gun.

Their personal effects were no better. Each soldier evidently had one uniform, a thin, loose shirt with long sleeves, buttoned up to the neck. They wore puttees wrapped over their trouser legs and leather boots. Some of them had lightweight sun helmets, but the majority wore a brown cap with a piece of cloth hanging down the back to protect the neck from the sun. Without exception the soldiers smelt to high heaven. The cheap cotton uniforms, once a dark tan, were faded to a dirty gray and stank with stale sweat. Long before you saw a Jap coming, you could smell him.

Their first move was to take all the government cars that were left in the city. Of the 150,000 troops that came through Batavia, only 30,000 stayed as an occupation force. The others were on their way to Bandung, so they grabbed any vehicle which would take them there faster.

I pedaled along the street on my bicycle, trying to look unconcerned, but keeping a sharp eye on everything that went on. The stinking Japs were everywhere. I saw three Japs jump off their bicycles and stop a car, moving through the densely packed street ahead of me. They gestured with their thumbs to show the native driver that they wanted the car and, when he hesitated, took him by the neck and threw him into the street. They tied their bicycles to the back of the car, took branches from a near-by tree and arranged them over the top to camouflage it. I was to learn that this act of camouflaging the car was typical of the Jap soldiers. Of course, such a precaution was unnecessary, as the Japs were masters of the air. But they are like machines. They had been told: "Whenever you ride in a car, be sure to camouflage it." So they did, without thinking whether it was necessary or not. But right there, I want to say that the Jap soldiers are excellently trained. The ones I saw had been fighting in China for four years and were the pick of the storm troops. They knew their job.

I didn't get far on my bicycle. Soon after the incident of the car, a Jap riding past me on his bicycle got a flat tire. Immediately he jumped to the ground and stopped me by wheeling his machine across my path. The soldier waved toward my bicycle, grinned and then pointed to his nose. For a moment I was puzzled, but finally his gestures, first toward my bicycle and then toward his nose, told me that this meant he was appropriating my machine. The motion toward his nose I was to see duplicated many times in the next months. It was the Jap way of indicating himself. "I," he would say with a gesture to his nose, "want this or that." A wise man gave it to him.

In spite of how I felt about everything that day, I couldn't help but be amused by the Jap as he tried to mount my bicycle. I am over six feet tall and my bicycle was large. This soldier was even smaller than many of his comrades. I watched him try to mount into the saddle, but he couldn't make it by the usual method. His legs were too short. He had to give an awkward jump to reach the seat and, once there, had the devil of a time balancing the machine. He finally solved the problem by standing up and leaning way over to one side to reach one pedal and then swaying back to the other side to propel the opposite one. I felt a little more cheerful as I watched him zigzagging a wobbly course down the street. He didn't look much like a world conquerer on that bicycle.

On the whole the occupation went smoothly. The Japs were careful to keep a crowd from forming and, even when some apprehensive natives got out small Jap flags and waved them about in hopes of pleasing the invaders, the soldiers disbanded them. They weren't sure how the natives or whites were going to react to their coming and any kind of crowd made them nervous. But there wasn't much resistance. All civilians were ordered by our government to stay at their jobs and to refrain from hostilities. A couple of natives got slapped by Jap soldiers when they started to protest the stealing of their bicycles, but most people didn't dare object.

When I reached my office, I was surprised to find that none of the Jap troops had been there. Word had gone around that the Japs had lists of all the government offices, the consulates, and business firms and were to take them over immediately. No one did much work that morning. We all felt nervous and wondered when the Japs would show up to occupy the office.

We didn't have long to wait. At noon a car carrying a Jap officer drove into the yard with soldiers carrying guns and bayonets riding on the running board. Accompanied by an armed guard, he went immediately to the head office. A few minutes later word came that all the employees of our division were to gather to hear a proclamation by the Jap officer.

As soon as we were all collected, the officer, a nervous man with the inevitable spectacles, began to talk rapidly in a sort of sing-song voice. He spoke Japanese, so I didn't understand a word of his speech. When he had finished, he gestured to one of his subordinates and this man repeated the officer's words in careful, precise English. What he said in substance was that this office was being taken over by the Japanese Government, that all of us were to work for them now and to keep on with our regular duties as though nothing had changed. Acts of sabotage, passive resistance or any forms of insubordination would be punished by death. He finished by saying that anyone who did not wish to abide by this new system would kindly step forward and declare himself.

The armed guards fixed their bayonets and waited. No one moved. I wondered if they expected anyone to announce his real feelings in the face of that barrage of steel.

The English speech over, another Jap repeated the same thing in Malayan for the benefit of our native employees. It had the same effect as the previous announcement. None of them was inclined to state his reaction to it by impaling himself on a Jap bayonet.

This formula completed, the officer sent some of his men about the building to paste up posters saying that the office was now the "Property of the Japanese Empire" and would be run for the benefit of "Greater Asiatic Prosperity."

I stayed to hear what else the Jap officer had to say. The first thing he did, when the majority of the employees had been sent back to their posts, was to draw his sword and show it to us. It was splashed with a brown stain from hilt to point.

"Anzac," declared the officer proudly, pointing to the dried blood. He meant that the blood was that of New Zealand and Australian soldiers he had killed in Malaya. Obviously this sword with its bloody stains was his most treasured possession.

After this display of vanity, the officer got down to business. He began asking innumerable questions about the office; how it was run, how many employees we had, the cost of maintaining it and so forth. Our chief answered briefly, but whenever he tried to evade a question, the officer supplied the answer himself. That's how well the Jap spies who had been living in Java had done their work. The officer already knew all about the company.

Toward the end of the interview the chief told the officer that he had two thousand Indonesian workmen and that two of them had been fired the week before, because, as he put it, "they did not wish to co-operate with our policies." He meant that these men had been Jap sympathizers and had been spreading propaganda, trying to make the rest of us see the glory that awaited us when the Japs took Java.

This news didn't seem to bother the Jap officer at all. He merely shrugged his shoulders and said, "Good." Of course, he knew that they couldn't run the office without our help and they needed to keep the public utilities going.

By this time more Jap officers had showed up and with them a strong force of sentries. The latter were immediately posted about the building, inside and out, and stood at their places with bayonets fixed. It was then that we first learned about bowing to the sentries. Everyone, white or native, had to bow as he passed one of the guards anywhere in the city. There wasn't much danger of our not finding out about this, as a sentry yelled, "Bow, bow," whenever he saw anyone of the "conquered races" approaching. Later we were given official regulations in the newspapers about this bowing. The men were to bow sixty degrees, the women forty-five degrees. The papers put it this way: "Citizens will bow to all sentries to show their respect for the protection the great Japanese Empire is giving them."

Naturally a lot of trouble came from this. It's easy to imagine that no white man wants to bow to a Jap, but we knew it would be foolish to refuse. There was nothing we could do about it; we had the choice of bowing or being run through with a bayonet. A dead man is no good to Holland and a wise man did as he was told under the circumstances. But the natives had a worse time with their bows. Most Javanese are Mohammedans and wear a small black cap as a sign of their faith. The Dutch government has always been careful to respect the native beliefs and of course never forbade the Indonesians to wear their caps.

But the Jap sentries were annoyed when they saw the natives bowing with their caps on and tried to knock them off. The Japs have a way of snarling, when they are angry, a hoarse, guttural sound, that betrays their bestial qualities. They would shout at the natives, beat them with their rifle butts and kick them to make them remove their caps. It didn't make the Indonesians feel any better about co-prosperity.

I learned before the day was over that the soldiers who had come to our office were the economic troops. Many of them were not professional soldiers at all, but businessmen who had been delegated to take over all industries and offices in Java. Each had been assigned to manage a certain office or plant and knew in advance almost as much about the business as our Dutch officials did. Before we went home, each one of us was given a band to wear on the left arm. It was printed in Japanese characters and said in effect that the wearer was working for the Japanese Government and was not to be molested in any way. We were instructed to wear these armbands all the time and not to remove them, if we valued our own safety.

When I went home that night I saw from the posters on

almost every office building that the economic troops had not been wasting time. All these posters bore the same announcement: that the concern was now the property of the Japanese Government and was to be run for the greater good of "Asiatic Prosperity." The posters made me wonder who was going to "prosper" by this wholesale exchange of ownership.

Once again in the midst of the sorrow and depression that had taken control of me, I saw something that amused me. As I've already said, the Jap soldiers were filthy with dirt and sweat by the time they reached Batavia and one of the first things they wanted to do was get clean. They went about this in a very direct manner. Without any hesitation they walked into someone's house and announced that they had come to use the bathroom. Of course, no householder was willing to dispute this under the circumstances, so the soldiers were given the free use of the bath. Friends of mine, who were subjected to an odorous visitation of this kind, told me that the Japs spent a couple of hours scrubbing themselves. After they were clean, they washed their uniforms. Without waiting for them to dry, the soldiers walked away, carrying their wet uniforms and wearing only a short white shirt that came just above their knees and was tied about the waist with a rope. It was the sight of these bandy-legged little men in their underwear that made me smile, though for obvious reasons I was careful to hide my amusement. The soldiers went everywhere in this scanty costume that first day; into stores, theaters, and on the street. It didn't help hide their physical shortcomings.

When I reached home I found three Jap soldiers in my

backyard, trying to pump water from the well. Seeing me, they began pointing to their noses in the usual way to indicate "I."

"Water, water," they said, gesturing to the well and then holding their noses. "Please, please."

I gave them water.

"Thank you, thank you."

While I stood watching them drink, they kept smiling and ducking their heads to me. Right then I got an idea that many of the Jap soldiers are somewhat in awe of white men. These men seemed to have a certain respect for me, perhaps because of my height, and were extremely polite. After they finished drinking, they took small tin pans from their packs and some rice. Squatting on the ground, they began eating.

"How far Bandung?" asked one.

I told him about a hundred and ten miles.

He sighed and made a hopeless gesture. "I walk," he said mournfully.

They went away soon after. My first encounter with Jap soldiers wasn't unpleasant. But it was hell to think that Java had been taken by ragged, half-starved men like these.

CHAPTER FIVE

WITHIN a week the Jap troops had taken over all the military barracks in town and had quartered their troops in them. Any building that the Japs wanted they took. If one of the larger office buildings was earmarked for occupancy by the economic troops, the financial experts, or any of the special soldiers, it was emptied immediately of its former tenants. These people and all those occupying houses near by were given three hours to vacate. Everything must be left behind for the use of the newcomers. Householders had to abandon all their furniture and personal possessions. All they were allowed to take with them was their clothes. The Japs had made no plans for establishing these people elsewhere. They were merely told to get out and it was up to them to find quarters in another section of the city or with their friends.

By this time the thirty thousand Jap soldiers who were to stay in Batavia had all arrived and their comrades had gone on to Bandung. Bandung had fallen three days after the surrender of Batavia. It was a natural stronghold, but the overwhelming numbers of Jap ground troops and the air superiority over our defenders were too much. They were our crack troops. Hour after hour they were strafed and bombed. Not a friendly plane was in the air. For three days they held out, then the Japs broke through the outer defense lines and Bandung capitulated. Now the entire island of Java was in the hands of the Japs.

The news from Bandung was bad enough, but it was worse to watch what was going on in our immediate vicinity. A few days after the initial occupation forces arrived in Batavia, the Kempei came to take control of the city. The Kempei is the police force modeled after the Gestapo. It is the real power in the Japanese Army and nothing the economic department does is of any use, unless the Kempei approves. The economic troops had done their work of taking over the business and government offices and now the Kempei appeared to rule Batavia. They were the real soldiers, tough, cruel, and war-hardened. It wasn't long before we knew the extent of their power.

They had prepared lists of all the important people in town, the police officials, businessmen, and government employees. In spite of the fact that the economic department had issued armbands to all these men, the Kempei picked them up and threw them in jail. Those they didn't bother with—and I was among them—were given another armband, this one with a special Kempei seal. The Kempei operated on the theory that everyone was guilty until proved innocent and they weren't taking any chances. These well-known Batavians were regarded as potential sources of insurrection, and all of them, whatever their position or importance to the functioning of government or business, were put in prison for safekeeping. There must have been three or four thousand men jailed at this time.

I was at the office when they came to take the chief and several of the department heads to jail, less than a week after they had been issued armbands by the economic officials. About fifteen or twenty soldiers entered the office, drew their swords and raised their guns, looking very serious and formal about the whole thing. Their commander told the chief that he must come with them. When he protested and pointed to his armband, the Jap officer snarled and made a threatening gesture with his sword. The guard moved closer. There was nothing for the chief to do. He went along with the guard.

Occasionally these armed guards took along a native policeman, one who had been retained in the police force and made to work for the Japs, when they went to get a man from his house. The policeman was very apologetic about it and hated having to work for the Japs.

"Please do not be angry," he would say to the householder, "but I must ask you, is the master of the house at home?"

If the answer was no, he said, still very meekly, "Please, may we look? Do not be angry please."

This wholesale jailing didn't please the economic department at all. They were trying to keep business and the utilities running as smoothly as possible, and this sweeping activity on the part of the Kempei was ruining their plans. As soon as our heads of the public utilities had been taken off to jail, things began to go wrong. The Jap officers in charge knew very little about technical problems and soon ran into trouble.

An instance of their difficulty serves as an illustration and a rather amusing one. One evening the Japanese general in charge of Batavia was entertaining a delegation of important Arab dignitaries at his office. Suddenly all the lights went out. The general flew into a rage and sent a hurry call for the Kempei officer in charge of the power plant. The officer knew nothing about a power plant or how to run one and, after being kicked around by the general for some time, went back to try to locate the trouble. But it was some hours before he could get the lights working and, in the meantime, the general and his guests sat in darkness.

Incidents like this increased the friction between the economic forces and the Kempei. The economic people were constantly trying to get the men they needed released from jail and the Kempei stubbornly refused to hurry themselves about it.

From what I was able to understand of the Kempei's action, they were chiefly interested in keeping as few troops as possible in Java. They had other fields to conquer and wanted to use their soldiers for fighting, not as occupation forces. They knew that the Europeans were a great source of danger as instigators of sabotage or a possible uprising. So they jailed them to keep them out of harm's way. Then, too, they realized it was to their advantage to try to erase the Dutch influence from Java. If they could show the natives that the Japs were more powerful than the white men, they hoped to make the Indonesians feel better disposed toward them. With most of the important Dutch businessmen and officials in jail, they would be out of touch with the natives and less able to influence them with counter-propaganda.

After the fall of Bandung the Kempei were busy collecting military prisoners. These they put in internment camps in the interior where, from all reports, they were treated very badly. I remember the Japs announcing that they had jailed 838 Americans. These were men who had been unable to get away when the British boats came to

Chilachap on the south coast to evacuate the Allied troops.

Some of these white prisoners of war received particularly rough treatment from their captors. In order to demonstrate to the natives how low the mighty white race had fallen, they put these military prisoners to work in the dirtiest part of town, cleaning out the gutters with their bare hands. But this childish propaganda had quite the opposite effect on the population. Once when I was passing a street corner where some of these poor devils were working at their disgusting job, I heard some natives talking among themselves. "*Kassian*," they repeated over and over again. They meant that it was a shame to see men working this way. Their only reaction was one of sympathy, not the general rejoicing that the Japs hoped to see.

We heard all kinds of stories about the treatment prisoners received, but it wasn't until the economic department finally persuaded the Kempei to release some people whose assistance they needed that I got a firsthand account of what went on in a Jap jail.

The prisoners were put in cells supposed to hold one man, but five or six were jammed into each one. They were given a thin mat to sleep on, one meal a day of rice and water and, worst of all, no mosquito nets. Occasionally they were allowed to walk up and down the corridor, but most of the time they had to stay in the cells. Whenever a Jap soldier came near, they had to bow and then stand at attention. If the soldier didn't like the way one of the men bowed, he would kick and slap him. Since most of these prisoners were important men, the Kempei supposed that they had special information that would be of value and they tried to get it out of them. They used third-degree methods to do this and several of the prisoners had been made to stand for hours before a group of questioners, getting slapped, kicked, and pushed around, if they couldn't or wouldn't answer a question. Of course many of the prisoners had nothing useful to tell the Japs, but the Kempei thought they must know something and kept on working at them.

One man committed suicide after being in prison a couple of days. He had some sleeping tablets and took an overdose of them. After that the Japs took everything away, any kind of bottle, razors, or belts. They didn't want anyone to get the impression that the prisoners weren't being treated right. Stories of suicides in the jails wouldn't stand comparison with the tales the Japs spread around of how humanely and kindly they treated all their prisoners.

The Jap economic experts tried to organize the food situation, but of course our regular market system was completely disrupted. The first few days after the occupation I could get nothing but rice and corned beef and this was food I happened to have in the house. All the stores were closed, the people who usually brought vegetables from the country never came near the city if they could help it, and the Japs closed the godowns or warehouses. The native population depends on rice, so they had the worst of it.

Shortly after the godowns were closed and a strong armed guard set to watch them, a group of starving natives tried to storm the warehouses. The Japs soon put a stop to that. They got a hollow tom-tom which the natives used for communication in the interior and set it up in a central square. When they had collected a large crowd by beating on it, they seized a few men and dragged them to a platform in the middle of the square. Then with three strokes of a double-edged sword (one under the jaw, one to the side, and a final blow) they decapitated the men. An officer announced that this was what happened to people who stole from the Japanese Army. The heads were placed on poles in the square with signs attached saying that such was the fate of those who did not work for "Greater Asiatic Co-prosperity."

We had other examples of this co-prosperity. The natives were naturally extremely nervous and uncertain about their status under Jap rule. Just before the occupation they had listened to Japanese propaganda broadcasts, explaining that they were of the same racial strain, the same color, and how they would help the natives gain control of Java for themselves. Many of the natives were half-inclined to hope that there was something in this, but they were soon disillusioned. While the Japs imprisoned many white men and treated them badly in jail, they seldom molested a European who was left free to walk the streets. But their treatment of the natives was uniformly bad. In spite of all their propaganda about "Asia for the Asiatics" and "Co-prosperity," their practice and their preaching were widely disparate. Just a few instances of their behavior toward the natives will suffice to show how they failed to live up to their propaganda.

Immediately after the occupation the Japs established a curfew. Everyone was supposed to stay off the streets between the hours of six in the evening and six in the morning. This curfew lasted for a month, until the Kempei had established "order." Naturally there were innumerable violations of the curfew and it was the natives who got punished for it. If one of them was caught on the streets during the forbidden hours, the Jap soldiers would draw a circle in the middle of the road and force the native to squat within it for twelve hours without moving. But this was one of the milder punishments.

They had fancier treatment for more important transgressions, such as not bowing low enough before a sentry, stealing a bit of rice, or walking on the wrong side of the street. These unfortunates received no mercy whatsoever. One punishment was to cut off their hands and tie them to trees to show others what happened to offenders of the Jap rule. Another system was that of tying a rope loosely about a man's neck and fastening him to a tree or pole in the street. No food or water was given him and after two or three days, the man would faint from weakness and automatically hang himself. Hundreds of natives died this way, miserable victims of Jap brutality.

The ordinary Jap soldiers seemed to enjoy mistreating the natives. They felt a certain awe of white men and would even duck their heads and grin when they met a European, but the natives had to bear the brunt of their savagery. They slapped and kicked them, shoved them about with the butt ends of their rifles at the slightest excuse and often for no excuse at all. One reason for this, as I came to see it from watching the Jap troops, is that the common soldiers get very rough treatment from their own officers. Whenever an officer wants to punish one of his men, he gets him up in front of his fellows and slaps him as a lesson to all of them. I saw one soldier standing at attention in the street while an officer yelled at him, slapping and kicking him continuously. The soldier's glasses fell off and the officer crushed them into the ground with his heel. Naturally the soldiers want to take it out on someone else, so they mistreated the natives and enjoyed doing it.

As a rule, the ordinary soldiers seemed to have no conception of the fact that their behavior didn't jibe with the Japanese propaganda with which they hoped to secure the goodwill of the Javanese. They treated the natives unmercifully, even while the radios, newspapers, and posters blared forth the fact that the coming of the Japs was bringing "Peace, goodwill and co-prosperity" to all Asia. But the officers were more intelligent. They seemed to make a conscious effort to bring some sort of agreement between their deeds and words. I never saw an officer kicking or slapping a native just for the mere joy of doing so. They punished them for offenses against their laws, but never just as an outlet for brutality.

I began to be interested in what the Japs thought about, what made them behave as they did. Though I hated every last one of the vicious little men, I wanted to find out what made them tick.

CHAPTER SIX

I DECIDED to learn Japanese. Since the vast majority of soldiers, and officers too, spoke only their native tongue, I had to learn their language if I wanted to talk to them. I've always been fairly quick at languages, but Japanese is a science in itself. I put myself on a strict regime of one hundred Jap "characters" a day and struggled to get a grasp of their intricacies. Soon I had a list of words at my command and began practicing them on the Jap soldiers and officers.

The first question I asked was what they thought about the war, what they hoped to get out of it. I was not long in discovering that most of them thoroughly enjoyed fighting and looked upon war as the only real way for a man to live. The basis for this belief is easy to understand; most of the common soldiers had led a miserable life at home. They were of the lowest order; ignorant, poverty stricken, and with nothing to look forward to except grinding work and slow starvation. Army life to them was seventh heaven; they had a bowl of rice a day, a uniform, and nothing to worry about. Their military leaders have crammed into their heads the idea that the only way to improve their lot at home is to go out and conquer the world. This they are fully confident they can do.

As I have already said, the Japs in Java were those who had already been fighting for four years in China. They were war-toughened, excellently trained in their business, and fanatical to an unbelievable degree. Only one or two soldiers showed me pictures of their wives and children and expressed a wish that the war was over so that they might go home. The others, the vast majority, wanted nothing better than a life of continual warfare. These latter were the true fanatics.

Once, talking to a group of soldiers who were off duty, I asked them what they would do if they were taken prisoner. They looked at me as though they thought I had lost my mind. No true son of the Empire, replied one in effect, would allow himself to be captured. He would kill himself first. From the look in his eyes as he spoke I knew he meant what he said.

Another told me very solemnly that he would never dare go home if he were taken prisoner or surrendered. His mother, he assured me, would spit on him for disgracing the family. Then his only course would be to commit *hara-kiri* in order to restore the family honor. He showed me with a gesture of his bayonet just how he would do this.

On the whole the Jap soldiers are extremely polite when talking to a white man. They always saluted before speaking and their conversation was riddled with "sorry" and "please," the two English words that most of them knew. They bowed and ducked their heads constantly and in general acted like schoolboys being addressed by a bishop.

Some of them know a few words of English and a little Malayan. But in talking to them I had to rely chiefly on my own poor knowledge of Japanese and gestures. The Japs can express almost any thought or action by a series of complicated motions of their hands and arms. I grew quite adept in this "deaf and dumb" language myself and soon could ask a soldier how he liked the war by pointing to him, then to his bayonet and finally by making the motion of stabbing someone with it. The Japs were highly amused by my efforts and always knew what I meant.

It was particularly interesting to hear what questions they asked me. The first one in almost every case was, "What about America?" Evidently America had been held up to them as the real enemy and they seemed apprehensive of the part the United States might play in the war. Often I was asked if I thought the Americans would bomb Japan. They had a very real fear that America would upset their apple cart, though in the light of events thus far, they had no reason to feel this way.

They had just taken the Philippines, Malaya, Borneo, and all the islands of the Indies and were extremely scornful of the Allied defense of these places. They felt that these campaigns had been easy for them, and the fact that Singapore, supposedly the strongest fortress in the world, had fallen so quickly was a source of great satisfaction to them. I often heard them joking about the American and British soldiers, and they evidently felt themselves to be so superior that there was no possible comparison. But they had a very healthy respect for the Chinese. One soldier expressed it by sticking up his thumb and saying, "Good, good," several times. They had been fighting the Chinese long enough to know what they were talking about.

When the soldiers were off duty they acted like children on a holiday. They were full of animal good spirits and seemed to have an inexhaustible supply of energy. One day a group of soldiers stopped me in the street and one of them suggested that we wrestle. But I had heard enough about *jujitsu* to know that I would be no match for him, in spite of the fact that I was twice his size. I knew too that, if I should happen to hurt him at all or made a false move that he felt injurious to his dignity, almost anything could happen. Getting run through with a bayonet might easily be the end of the wrestling match for me. I wanted to stay on their good side in any case and always pretended a friendliness toward them. It would do me no good to get in their bad books.

When I declined to wrestle with him the soldier took my refusal in good part, but immediately suggested I sing an American jazz song. Before I could make my excuses, he began gesturing as though playing a guitar and singing in a hoarse, guttural voice the English words to "Dinah." His friends accompanied this exhibition by doing a clumsy imitation of an American dance. They were delighted with their own performance and repeated it several times.

On the whole I discovered that the majority of the common soldiers are totally ignorant of everything but the mechanics of war and a smattering of Japanese history. They have been told that Japan's destiny is to rule Asia and the Pacific and they believe this wholeheartedly. They know nothing of what goes on in other countries, and foreign nations to them are peopled by savages who want to wipe Japan off the face of the earth. This fear of the outside world is pumped into them as part of their fighting equipment.

As their treatment of the natives proves, they are inherently brutal, cruel and take a savage delight in maltreating those who cannot strike back. The only reason most Europeans escaped their tyranny is that they were bigger than the Japs. Then, too, as I have already suggested, the common soldier has an innate respect for a white man that no amount of propaganda can overcome.

The officers are quite different from the troops. They are better educated, naturally, have a wider knowledge of world affairs and a broader cultural background. Nonetheless they are just as certain in their belief in Japan's "manifest destiny." Their whole way of thought is directed toward one end: to make Japan a world power.

Their fanaticism is equally strong. War is man's natural state of being and the only worth-while honor one can gain in this world is through fighting. One showed me a wound he had received in the Malayan battles. Half his chest was torn by shrapnel and he was enormously proud of this badge of courage. Another showed me his sword, covered with dried blood. He said that it was the blood of "hundreds" he had slain. The sword had been in his family's possession for generations and it was his most treasured possession.

The officers spoke better English and many of them talked with scarcely the trace of an accent. The men of the economic department were particularly well educated and had a wide knowledge of their jobs and matters of general information.

The officers did their best to offset the brutality of the soldiers. If they caught a man mistreating anyone, particularly being rude or overbearing to a white person, they would interfere immediately. An instance of this happened to a girl I know in Surabaya.

She was riding in a crowded street car when a group of Jap soldiers got on. They immediately pushed their way toward her and demanded that she give one of them her seat. This girl was not used to such treatment and, being Dutch, was as stubborn as only a woman or a mule can be. She flatly refused to get up.

"I wouldn't get up for a Dutchman and I'm damned if I'll get up for a Jap," she announced.

The soldiers began kicking her feet and one of them slapped her several times. She still refused to move. Then another snatched her handbag and tossed it out the window. This only served to make her more determined than ever to stay where she was.

What might have happened to her next can only be imagined, for the car stopped and two Jap officers got on. They immediately saw what was going on and ordered the trolley to stop. Then they grabbed the soldiers and tossed them out into the street. One of them walked back to pick up the handbag. After slapping and kicking the soldiers to teach them a lesson, the officers came back to the girl and apologized profusely. "Sorry, so sorry. Excuse please," they repeated over and over again.

Other incidents of the officers' efforts to counteract the behavior of the troops occurred when the soldiers stole anything, either from the people or from shopkeepers. It appeared that every Jap's greatest wish in the world was to own a watch. Before they had been in Batavia a week, every jewelry store in town was bare of watches. The soldiers had a very simple method of acquiring these time-pieces. They would enter a shop, point out a watch to the clerk and announce that they wanted it. Occasionally they paid less than the asking price in Japanese script, but more often they merely walked off without so much as a thank you.

When the officers realized the soldiers were doing this, they announced that every watch was to be returned immediately. They accompanied the men back to the stores and insisted that the watches be given back or else paid for in full in script. The fact that the script was practically worthless made no difference. To the officers it was the principle of the thing. The soldiers weren't supposed to steal and the officers were there to see that they obeyed the letter of the law at least.

Petty pilfering went on all over the city, but whenever the officers heard about it they took measures to stop it. Friends of mine, men who had worked temporarily in Bandung, told me a story that illustrates the officers' efforts to keep peace between the soldiers and the people.

On their way home to Batavia my friends ran into a repair crew of Jap soldiers who were fixing one of the bridges that had been blown up by the retreating Dutch. They were stopped and told that everyone who passed that way must work two hours, helping to repair the bridge. There was no way out of it so they took off their coats and set to work. A Jap officer stood over the whole gang with a long whip and whenever he saw anyone, either a soldier or civilian worker, slacking a little, he uncurled his whip and let him have it across the shoulders.

While the men were working, two Jap soldiers came up and searched them, evidently looking for weapons. But instead of guns they took a wristwatch from one fellow and a pair of sun glasses from another. The men tried to protest, but were silenced by a menacing gesture with a bayonet.

At the end of the two-hour stretch they went up to the Jap officer to announce that they had finished their stint. The officer saluted them and said, "Thank you," very formally. He seemed quite civil and one of the men decided to mention the fact that his watch was gone. He had no sooner told him that the soldiers had taken the watch and sun glasses than the officer flew into a violent rage.

All the soldiers were made to form a line and the officer announced that the two who had taken the articles were to step forward and return them. The soldiers obeyed instantly and, with many apologies and hissing excuses, the officer returned the stolen property. The last my friends saw of the officer he was yelling at the two soldiers, slapping them in a fury of anger.

The officers were obviously sincere in their determination to make their propaganda have some meaning. They did their best to offset the bad effect of the soldiers' brutality and senseless mistreatment of the natives. But there weren't enough officers to catch all the offenders.

Perhaps as a means of keeping the soldiers out of mischief the officers kept them up to a strict military training. Every day between two and three in the afternoon, when the temperature is well over a hundred, the soldiers were made to run up and down the streets. They wore their heaviest uniforms and carried bayonets with which they practiced stabbing motions as they ran. The sweat poured off them, but they weren't allowed a moment's rest. From time to time they gave hoarse yells, a sort of animal cry. I learned that these shouts are part of their training. They are intended to frighten the enemy.

But it was by propaganda that the Japs hoped to conquer the Indonesians. Their slogans were meant to win them to the Japanese point of view, in spite of the daily evidences that the Japs had no understanding of or sympathy for the natives.

CHAPTER SEVEN

"*ASIA RAYA, Asia Melindung, Asia Pemimpin!*"

"Greater Asia, Cooperative Asia, Harmonious Asia!"

This slogan appeared everywhere—on posters, over the radio, and in the newspapers. The Japs drummed away at the idea that their coming was the greatest blessing ever bestowed on Java. They were determined that the Indonesians should forget the Dutch and everything that we had brought in the way of advancement.

But the natives had their own slogans. A few weeks of Jap occupation was enough to convince them that the way the "Three A's," as this principal rallying cry was termed, should really read was, "*Asia Raya, Nippon Kaya, Asia Paya.*" Translated as "Greater Asia, Richer Japan, Poorer Asia," it shows that no one was blind as to who was to benefit by the Japanese conquests.

Naturally the Japs took over all the newspapers and radio broadcasting stations immediately. Every newspaper plant was shut down within a week after the occupation and only a few Malayan papers were allowed to continue publication. Of course the Japs controlled these and filled them with their propaganda for native consumption. Their own newspaper, called *Greater Asia,* was their principal organ and in it they printed a fantastic array of lies, twisted tales, and glorified accounts of Jap conquests. Every battle in which their troops, ships, or planes was engaged anywhere on the globe was announced as a Japanese victory, no matter how many ships, planes, or men might have been lost. The losses weren't mentioned.

The Japs had brought correspondents from all their big news agencies and these men kept themselves busy dreaming up tall tales for home consumption about the glorious welcome the Jap troops had received from the "oppressed Indonesian people." They printed pictures of a Jap and a Javanese shaking hands while a dove of peace flew overhead. The natives might have found more meaning in this happy thought if the Jap soldiers hadn't expressed their peaceful intentions by cutting off their heads at the slightest provocation.

The radios blared from dawn to dusk on the same themes. No one had a chance to hear anything but the propaganda idea that the Japs and Javanese were the "same color, the same race." Within a few days of the conquest, special troops visited every house in Batavia to seal the short-wave radio bands, so that no one could listen to foreign broadcasts. Needless to say, there were many people among the Dutch population who disobeyed this edict and risked imprisonment or worse to get the news from outside.

One young fellow had a concealed radio to which he listened every night. The news he received he printed on a hand press and distributed among his friends. He was caught finally and we heard he had been shot. But we still got some outside information. The Indonesians who worked at the Jap radio stations often were able to pick up foreign broadcasts and they relayed what they heard to their friends. The truth travels fast and there were few people of any intelligence in Batavia who did not know a great deal of what was going on in the world.

I remember turning on my radio one night at ten o'clock about a week after the conquest and hearing, to my amazement, the Dutch National Anthem. Each night for a week this same thing happened. Evidently the Japs aren't very musical, for it took them all this time to catch on to what was happening. Two men who worked at the radio station had been playing a record of the anthem right under the noses of the enemy. It was a splendidly foolish thing for them to do, for, when the Japs finally realized what the tune was, the two men paid dearly for their loyalty. They were imprisoned for several weeks and later shot.

By way of erasing all evidence of Dutch influence, the Japs began changing the names of all the streets, shops, and buildings. It was fairly easy for them to go about putting up signs announcing that such and such a place was now to be known by a Japanese or Malayan name. But no one ever referred to them by the new terms. The Indonesians aren't people who can change customs quickly and, since they had no wish to forget the Dutch in any case, the Japs had little success with this campaign.

For some reason the Japs decided soon after they were established in Java that the terms Japan and Japanese were not to be used any more. Perhaps they felt that the name "Jap" by which everyone called them was detrimental to their dignity. In any event it was announced that from now on the conquerers of Java were to be called Nipponese and their country Nippon. Anyone violating this rule was liable to strictest punishment. But they had the same success with this idea as they had with the name changing of the streets and buildings. They were Japs to the Dutch and natives, and I never heard anyone call them Nipponese, unless he were face to face with one of them.

The movies also were converted to Jap propaganda uses. Every theater was closed soon after the occupation and only opened to show some special Jap film. These movies were the rankest propaganda, showing scenes of happy family life in the factories and fields of Japan or, more often, battle pictures of Jap conquest. Their favorite in the latter category was the attack on Pearl Harbor, which they announced had been totally destroyed. Every battle in which Jap forces participated was claimed as a "complete victory." I saw the film they showed of the Battle of the Coral Sea. The commentator declared that the whole American fleet had been sunk in this engagement.

The Japs had a hard time getting people to come to the theaters to watch films like these, even though they reduced the admittance fee to a mere fraction of what it had been in peace time. In order to make theater going more attractive, they released a few Hollywood pictures, but only ones that had been carefully censored. One that the Japs liked particularly was a fantasy called *1,000,000 B.C.*, a very mediocre picture by any artistic standards. But it showed white men acting like savages, eating with their fingers and living in caves, and, for this reason, the Japs considered it highly effective as anti-American propaganda.

Another American picture, *Seven Sinners*, was presented several times. I had seen it before the occupation and went again to find out what the Japs would do to it. Even before the picture began, an announcement was flashed on the screen saying, "This picture is *busuk* (rotten) because it shows ships of the American Navy that have been totally annihilated by the Imperial Japanese Navy." Throughout the showing an announcer interrupted to cry, *"Busuk!"* whenever he felt that the action required this comment. Much of the picture had been censored so that the story was completely ruined and made no sense whatsoever.

I heard that Charlie Chaplin's *The Great Dictator* was being shown to the Jap officers in Batavia, but we never saw it at a public theater. The rumor was that the officers enjoyed it tremendously and got a big laugh out of seeing their allies, Hitler and Mussolini, as portrayed by the Messrs. Chaplin and Oakie. In fact, they liked it so much it was repeated four or five times for their exclusive benefit.

Instead of turning the natives against America by showing such mutilated Hollywood products, it only served to increase the Indonesians' regard for that country. Like many people in the world, the Javanese have an almost awed respect for the great Western Democracy. They look upon it as a land of hope and promise where all the streets are paved with gold and the common man can live in ease and luxury. They know it to be a powerful country, and America to them is the nation that will finally release them from the power of the Japs. So confident are they of this that they originated a slogan which passed by word of mouth throughout Java. It is their own version of the "Three A's": *"Awas, Ada America!"* It means, "Beware, there is America!"

CHAPTER EIGHT

ABOUT a month after the Japs arrived, a huge fleet of troop transports appeared at Tandung Priok, the harbor of Batavia. Soldiers were loaded onto barges at the docks and taken out to larger ships in the outer harbor. Most of the troops who had actually participated in the battle for Java left at this time and a new contingent appeared to act as the occupying force. These new soldiers were so much like the others that we in Batavia scarcely noticed the change. There were men from the economic department to run business and industry and, of course, a large group from the Kempei to keep order. Though I never heard how many soldiers there were in this new occupation force, I should judge that there were several thousand in Batavia alone.

Life went on just as it had in recent weeks, though now the Japs began to bring some organization into their rule. They had tried to impress on everyone the fact that they had come to Java to stay, and, though neither the natives or whites believed this, the Japs went busily to work to implant themselves in the Indies.

As part of their effort to eradicate all Dutch influence from Java, they closed all the schools, both native and European. After some time they reopened the elementary schools only, with a new educational system for the natives. The Dutch language was forbidden in the schools; all the teachers had to conduct their classes in Malayan or Japanese. Since none of the instructors spoke Japanese, they were given a quick course in the language to prepare themselves for the new order. European teachers, whether Dutch or any other white race, were thrown out of the schools entirely. The schools were to be run for the exclusive benefit of the Indonesians, for the Japs had learned the obvious lesson that the most effective way to spread their doctrines was through the children. If a child was taught nothing but what the Japs wanted him to know, he would grow up a model member of a subject race.

Teaching the Japanese language was not only confined to the schools. Instructors appeared everywhere, even on street corners, and set up shop. Whether anyone listened to them or not, they went right ahead propounding the rules of Japanese grammar. The newspapers announced that everyone must make himself familiar with Japanese, for "This will be the future language of the world."

All letter writing was banned and the only postal communication allowed was by postcard—easy for the censors to read. These cards had to be written in Malayan or Japanese, for, as I have said, the Dutch language "no longer existed," according to the Japs. Occasionally, as a special treat, civilians were allowed to send packages of food and clothing to their relatives in the internment camps. The Emperor's birthday was considered an occasion for tremendous rejoicing, and the Indonesians and some Europeans were permitted to participate in the celebration by sending war prisoners a few necessities of life.

The principal thing these prisoners needed was medical supplies. We heard frightful stories of the way wounded soldiers were treated, or rather not treated. They had no bandages, medicines, or nursing care. A few Japanese doctors were supposed to look after them, but either there weren't enough of them or they didn't pay much attention to their jobs. The wounded prisoners were to all intents practically uncared for.

All the hospitals had been taken over and Jap doctors and nurses installed. The Dutch medical men were either interned or told to leave their work, though a few native doctors and nurses were made to stay on the job and help the Japs. The civilian population was just as badly off for medical attention as the prisoners, for all the hospitals were run for the Japanese Army. If any of us got sick we could only hope for the best. The Dutch doctors were handicapped in their work among the civilians by lack of supplies and, if an epidemic of any kind had struck us, there would have been nothing to check it.

The Japs now had control of all phases of life in Java. One of the most interesting proofs of their imitative habits was their administration of justice in the courts. Of course, they had taken over the judicial machinery immediately, but in the courts they made fewer changes than in other places. They were smart enough to realize that the Dutch system worked well and they didn't want to disrupt it. Many of the Dutch judges were forcibly retained and the Japs watched the way they meted out justice with great attention. They had always been respectful of our governmental administration and knew that, by watching the way we did things, they could learn a great deal.

The tax system, too, they left as it was. The Japs admitted that it was effective and that's the best that can be said of any tax collecting. But now the natives weren't making the wages they had under Dutch rule, and when the Japs tried to collect on the previous year's incomes, the Indonesians had nothing with which to meet the tax. Surprisingly enough, the Japs were lenient and gave them three months in which to try to find their tax money. Close imitation of the Dutch administration methods was one of the most ominous aspects of the Jap conquest to me. It showed that they had every intention of keeping Java and exploiting its riches.

The lowering of the wage scale which I have just mentioned was the point of greatest friction between the Japs and the natives. The Dutch had paid from seventy-five to eighty cents for an eight-hour day with overtime. The Japs paid them thirty-five cents a day and nothing for overtime. One man I knew asked for his overtime wage, after working a twelve-hour stretch, and was thrown into jail for a fortnight.

The native reaction to this wage cut was to quit work entirely. The Indonesians have a strong family feeling, and those who had jobs in the cities knew that all they had to do was to go home to their families in the mountain villages. Here they could be sure of a bowl of rice a day and, most important of all, harmonious surroundings, which to them is the most necessary thing in life. Any Indonesian would rather exchange a good job in the city paying anywhere from fifteen to twenty guilders a month for one paying little or nothing in his native village. Here he could be sure of harmony among his gentle, peace-loving relatives.

But the Japs had work to be done, repairing the demolished roads, buildings, and bridges destroyed by the Dutch Army, so they drafted native labor to speed it along. One method of their doing this came to my attention when one of our native boys at the office asked me if he could go home to visit his people for two days. I gave permission, but it was a month and a half before he returned. He was covered with bruises from head to foot and evidently had been mercilessly mistreated by the Japs. His story was that while walking to his village he passed by an airdrome that the Japs were rebuilding. They spotted him and immediately put him to work on the field. Here he was forcibly retained for several weeks, being locked in the airdrome at night, given no wages and very little food for his labor. If he tried to escape or showed signs of slacking on the job, he was beaten and kicked until he could hardly stand. He at last managed to get away one night, and, after reaching his family's house and receiving treatment, came back to Batavia.

His case was only one among thousands like it during the time I was there. Scarcely any of the natives worked willingly for the Japs, even those who had at first been influenced by the propaganda about the benefits they would receive under the Japs. The low wage scale, or, as more often happened, no wage at all, was enough to convince the natives that they were going to get nothing out of their new rulers.

Another important reason for the general state of unemployment among the natives was the wholesale closing down of most business offices. All the European firms that had once employed thousands of natives were out of business. The import and export houses, the consulates, the great agricultural estates had to shut up shop immediately after the occupation, since they were cut off from the world market. The Japs couldn't run them, as the majority of these firms had dealt with the Allied nations and naturally none of them were doing business with the Japs.

They made no attempt to keep these businesses going, as a matter of fact, because they didn't need them. By re-drilling they could get oil from Tarakan more easily than they could from Java, where the oil needed refining. Sugar, tea, rubber, and rice were plentiful in other places they had conquered. Until they had consolidated their gains in the Pacific, they were content to let Java's great natural resources remain unused. Java to them is chiefly valuable right now as a strategic naval and aviation base. The harbor at Surabaya is one of the largest in the world and they immediately set about rebuilding it with drafted native labor. The airdromes, of which we had ten scattered throughout the interior of the island, were quickly put into working condition again, also by native workers. New airports and naval construction work at Surabaya were begun. The Japs are fitting Java as a naval and air stronghold. That is the principal role that the island is to play in the Jap military scheme, at least for the time being.

Though the Indonesians had the worst of the new Jap "order" from every point of view, the white people were not much better off. True, they were seldom molested by the conquerors, except for the unfortunate businessmen and government officials who were jailed. The rest of us weren't important enough to bother with. I was protected by the Kempei armband which I was careful to wear everywhere and, since I did not have an executive job, I was not thought to be in a position to have any special knowledge that might be dragged out of me by third-degree methods.

I was not watched and was able to move about Batavia pretty much as I pleased. Of course there were restricted areas, such as the waterfront, where we weren't supposed to go. But, as I shall mention later, even forbidden spots like these were not always closely guarded.

The white women, too, were left strictly alone. Just before I left I heard that the Japs were going to set aside a certain area of Batavia for the exclusive use of the white women where they could live together without fear of harm. But this was not done while I was there and indeed there was no particular need for such a restricted area. Unlike some of the other countries conquered by the Japs, Java was not evacuated by the white women and children.

No Netherlander was allowed to leave the country and almost nobody wanted to. The Indies were our home; we had lived there with the Indonesians for so many years in prosperity, why should we run away when trouble came. The only people who escaped were those men who had orders from the Dutch government to leave before the occupation. The ones who left were men whose specialized knowledge and skill in a variety of fields were necessary to the war effort. Therefore, the large majority of the white families stayed on in Java when the Japs came. The natives had no cause to say, as we heard they did in other countries, that the whites had run out on them and left them to face the Japs alone.

Our greatest hardship was the lack of money. The Japs took over all the banks immediately and appropriated the funds they contained. Any money that we had on hand was exchangeable for Japanese script, but when this was gone many people had no further resources. The heads of many families were in jail and their wives and children were soon badly off. Not even pensions were paid and some had depended entirely on such money for a livelihood. Only those who worked for the Japs had any regular source of income. I had my salary, though now it was less than half what it had been. I was fortunate to be in a position to help some of my friends, and during the time I was in Java supported seven families on my wages.

With so many people in straitened circumstances everyone fell to and helped one another. Dutch and Chinese landlords agreed to forget the rents owed to them by many householders. "After the war," they said. "Then we will think about your rent." Those who had more money than others were generous with it and all shared and shared alike with their friends and relatives.

Those who had servants told them that they would have to leave, as there was no money to pay their wages any more. Invariably the native and Chinese servants responded by saying, "You don't have to pay us. Just give us a plate of rice every day so we have something to eat and we will stay." These people knew that they would be better off with a friendly employer even without wages, than shifting for themselves with the Japs.

The natives expressed great sympathy for the white people in their difficulty. I remember hearing one Indonesian say, as he saw a Dutch woman in the market picking out the cheapest foods, "It is a shame that you are in such a condition. I pity you." It was obvious that the "oppressed natives," as the Japs love to call them, were not rejoicing to see their former masters in such unhappy circumstances. They were sorry for them and felt none of the elation the Japs expected at being "freed" from Dutch rule.

Another reason why people had so little money was due to the registration cards we were forced to buy from the Japs. The cards stated one's age, race, and length of time in the Indies. They cost a white man one hundred and fifty guilders, a white woman eighty guilders. Chinese paid one hundred guilders for the cards and their women fifty guilders. This was a lot of money, but we had to have the cards or risk being thrown into jail.

Needless to say, our whole way of life was changed. We no longer had access to any of the amusements we had enjoyed during peace time. No one wanted to go to the movies more than once or twice. It was scarcely pleasant to see a Jap propaganda picture and the ordinary films were so distorted by censorship that they meant nothing. Formerly the white people had spent a good deal of their leisure time at the great hotels, dining or dancing, or at one or another of the clubs of which there are several famous ones in Batavia. But now the Hotel des Indes was occupied by Jap officers and no one else was allowed inside. These officers could be seen drinking and playing billiards through the hotel windows, and it was not a spectacle that made one want to join in the fun. The Harmonie, one of the largest of the men's clubs, was similarly used. All the former members were excluded and the Jap officers had the free run of the place.

Everyone stayed at home and the only relaxation we had was visiting among our friends. Occasionally the Japs would put on a show for the edification of the public. One of these was the burial service held at the Fair Grounds in the Konigsplein in commemoration of the Japs who had died in the Battle of Java. This was really quite impressive. Masses of soldiers lined up in the square, facing a platform draped with flags of the Rising Sun. A speaker addressed them, paying honor to the dead, and then the soldiers sang. This singing was what was most effective. One group at the back of the audience began the song and it was taken up by various other groups at different intervals. Finally the whole array of men was singing. I had always heard that Japanese singing was a monotonous singsong, but these soldiers sang in the Western manner. They have several rousing national songs and evidently are trained to sing them so that they get the most effect out of them. I was honestly impressed, not by what they were singing, but by the way in which they did it.

One of our favorite forms of relaxation was listening to rumors, either because we half hoped they were true or because they gave us something to talk about. The natives were generally the ones who started these stories and, while I knew none of them had any basis in fact, I hated to act the wet blanket by refuting them. A particularly persistent rumor was one that said the Americans were coming, that they would be in Java at any moment to deliver the island from the Japs. We were always hearing that American troops were even now in Bali or Sumatra or Borneo, getting ready for a big offensive against the Japs. As soon as one rumor proved itself to be false, another would spring up to take its place, a story equally as fantastic as the last, but always a source of hope and comfort to the natives. These tales helped preserve our morale, which, during the time I was in Java, was very good. People lived on the belief that this period of degrading conquest was only temporary and that some day the last Jap would be driven off the island.

There is a native legend in Java, in which the Indonesians put great faith. Hundreds of years ago some prophet said that one day Java would be overrun by yellow men from the north. These conquerors would control the island absolutely, but at the end of one hundred days they would be driven away. The hundred days had come and gone, however, and still the Japs had Java.

CHAPTER NINE

BUT I wasn't going to wait for any outside help to be delivered from Jap rule. Two weeks after the Japs took Java, I decided that I had had enough of "co-prosperity." I am young, just twenty-eight years old; I have no family. There was nothing of a personal nature to keep me there. It looked as though it would be a long time before the Dutch came back and I didn't want to wait that long and do nothing to help my country. The Japs were getting a firmer grip on the island with each passing day; they were smart, tough, and there were a lot of them. I didn't want to fight this war as a prisoner-in-all-but-name of the Japs.

Ever since I was a child I've owned a boat of some kind. As a hobby I've studied navigation and know the rudiments of this complicated science. Several years ago I captained a yacht for a wealthy man on a trip to Honolulu. I've sailed to most of the islands of the South Seas. Sailing and the sea are familiar to me and I knew that my one chance of escape was by boat. But where to get one now that the Japs were in control of the island was a problem that fairly staggered the imagination.

All yachts in the yacht basin at Tanjung Priok had been scuttled by the Japs, in order to prevent an escape like the one I was contemplating. Not a single ship of the original hundreds that had once graced the harbor remained in a usable condition. I know because I investigated the basin shortly after my plan began to take form.

I bicycled down to the waterfront at Tanjung Priok, some seven miles east of Batavia. The way lies along an inland waterway paralleling the sea wall on the shore. A straight road follows the river, which runs some hundreds of yards in from the sea. The intervening space between the road and sea is a flat marshy area, which has never been filled in or developed in any way and is almost completely deserted. Far away across this boggy marshland I could see a sentry patrolling the sea wall. He watched me as I pedaled along the road to Tanjung Priok, but made no motion to stop me.

Tanjung Priok is one of the largest harbors in the Indies. It is composed of several long piers, lying alongside each other, all of them covered by big godowns or warehouses. In peace time the docks were a lively place, teeming with activity, as the natives loaded the big cargo ships which made the harbor one of their chief ports of call. Now the entire area was dead. The warehouses were locked, the piers empty of life. The water was filled with the hulks of sunken ships, some of them scuttled by the Dutch before the army left Batavia and some the Japs had destroyed. It was a dreary, depressing sight.

The yacht basin was particularly distressing to me. All the beautiful little ships which had once made the harbor so lively lay submerged, their hulks waterlogged and only the outlines visible just below the surface. I had heard previously that the Japs had taken the masts and rigging off all the boats, before scuttling them, and stored this equipment in one of the godowns. But all the warehouses were locked and, even if by any remote chance I could have raised one of the sunken yachts, I would have had no hope of getting its sails and mast out of the godown.

I hadn't dared go too near the docks in making this hasty inspection of the yacht basin and I soon discovered that I had been wise to be cautious. I got off my bicycle and started to walk nearer the boats, when a Jap sentry suddenly jumped out from behind a godown and flourished his bayonet in my face. He snarled and waved me away. I didn't try to argue. I got on my bicycle and rode off. I knew then that there was no hope of getting a boat from the yacht basin. They were in no condition to be made ready for sailing and were too closely guarded to make any attempt to raise one either feasible or sensible. I would have to look somewhere else.

On my way back I looked along the riverfront more carefully. This region between Tanjung Priok and Batavia along the river is closely packed with small warehouses and docks, most of them the home ports of the native fishing boats or *prahus*, as they are called. The Chinese own most of these docks and before the Japs came had done a flourishing trade there. Now only a few of them were doing a desultory business with the fishermen. The Japs had not forbidden the natives to fish, though they watched all the *prahus* that went out very closely and supervised their activity as they did everything else in Java.

I saw the masts of several *prahus* over the tops of the godowns as I rode back toward Batavia, and a faint hope began to stir within me. I knew that a *prahu* would not do for the kind of trip I had in mind; the native boats are too small and frail for anything but sailing about near the shore. But I wondered if the Japs might not have over-looked a larger boat somewhere in the maze of docks, warehouses, and piers in this district. The whole area was filled with small shipping. An apparently harmless little ketch or cutter might have been passed over as not worth their trouble by the Japs when they destroyed most of the boats in the harbor. I rode more slowly, peering intently over the roofs of the warehouses, always hoping to see the varnished mast which would tell me that a sturdier boat than a *prahu* was located there. The native boats all have unfinished masts, mere poles to support the big sails.

But I didn't dare go too near the riverfront then to make an inspection. The Jap sentries, spaced at regular intervals along the sea wall, were watching me and I didn't want to make them suspicious. I went home that day having seen nothing that would give me any hope of following out my plan of escape. For already I knew where I must go and the course I must follow to get there.

I have sailed the Indian Ocean countless times and I know its winds and weathers as well as anyone can know such uncertain elements. The distance from Batavia to Australia is some 1200 miles, but each foot of the way is against the prevailing trade winds which sweep from the southeast. From Batavia to Colombo on the island of Ceylon is roughly 1800 miles. Here again the winds would work against me, for throughout this region are the doldrums, areas where the winds, if they blow at all, are squally or so light that sailing is mere guesswork. My best chance lay to the southwest to the island of Rodriguez, just east of Madagascar, over three thousand miles across the Indian Ocean. I would have the trade winds to help me all the way. In spite of the greater distance, I decided that it was to Rodriguez that I would set my course, when and if I found a boat to take me there.

It was a month before I found the boat I wanted. During this time I made frequent trips to the waterfront, but I had always to be careful. The sentries were everywhere and I knew that if they saw me in the district too often, they would begin to get suspicious. I was so fortunate, however, as to be given more outside work to do; inspection trips and other jobs that offered me a good excuse for absenting myself from work so often. Thus, if I were stopped by a sentry, I could tell him that I was at the waterfront on business.

No one at the office or among my friends had any idea of my plans. I realized that the less said about my scheme the better. Even the most sympathetic person might let something slip unintentionally and then it would be a concentration camp for me. It was safer to tell no one; certainly not until my plans had matured and I needed help in getting away.

I saw the little ketch one afternoon moored in the fishing harbor at Batavia. It lay near the yacht club, just below the lookout tower by one of the river drawbridges. Why the Japs had overlooked this ketch, I never knew. Its masts and sails were gone, it was half filled with water. But when I saw it, my spirits rose as though on wings. This was the boat I had been looking for. There were no sentries about, except for a group in the lookout tower. A hasty glance assured me that these men were too busy lazing away the afternoon playing cards and sleeping to pay heed to me.

No one saw me as I gave the boat a quick inspection. There was an auxiliary engine; its hull was in good shape, well made and entirely seaworthy. In the cabin I found an old sea chart of the Sunda Strait, the passage between Java and Sumatra, which we would have to go through to reach the Indian Ocean. I took it, for it would be invaluable to me in navigating this narrow waterway.

I didn't dare linger near the boat too long. But within a few moments I knew what I would need to outfit the ketch; a complete set of sails, spars and rigging and a mast. Where I could get all this equipment I had no idea, but, as I rode away, I was too elated to worry about anything. Even the appalling problem of working on the boat in its exposed position did not present too many difficulties at that time. Something could be arranged, I felt sure. Perhaps I could move the boat some night to a safer place at one of the Chinese docks on the riverfront. Or perhaps the sails, mast, and so forth could be made at home and rigged on the boat at the last minute.

Now that I had found my boat, there were a multitude of problems to face. I must have food for the trip, at least enough for fifty days at sea. With luck I might make the voyage in a shorter time, but I wanted to be on the safe side. I needed instruments—a chronometer, a sextant, a nautical almanac, charts, and various hand tools. All these things, in addition to the first necessities of a mast, sails, and rigging, presented terrific difficulties. But I was determined not to be discouraged. I must get away and nothing was going to stop me.

Still another question faced me. I knew I could never make the trip alone. I needed at least two other men to help me get that boat across the Indian Ocean. Where could I find men willing to take the risks the whole plan entailed? None of my friends were in a position to leave; they had families or other responsibilities which would keep them in Java. I must find my companions somewhere and they would have to be chosen carefully. At the moment I knew no one whom I dared approach with my scheme.

Meanwhile I busied myself in collecting some of the needed supplies. Since all the shops were closely watched by the Japs, I couldn't buy the nautical equipment just by going to a store and asking for it. I would have to get it piecemeal from the black market or from people who had once owned boats and might have some things they had salvaged before their ships were scuttled. It was easier to concentrate on the food first, so I began laying in a hoard of rice, corned beef, canned fruits, and vegetables. I could get only a few things at a time, as canned goods were scarce and buying in quantity would arouse suspicion.

In a secondhand shop I found an old sextant which I was able to purchase by saying that I was studying navigation as a hobby and needed it in my work. The Chinese owner merely shrugged as he sold it to me. Perhaps he knew I had other plans, but he wasn't going to question me. The chronometer was harder to find. I saw one in a pawn shop, but the Japs were running it now and I didn't dare go in and ask for it. For the time being the chronometer would have to wait.

I had decided to make my own sails for the ketch and was lucky enough to get a piece of canvas from a friend, who asked no questions and pretended to believe my story that I was going to make myself a pup tent. I made frequent visits to the harbor to see if the boat was still there and had the satisfaction of finding that the little ketch was apparently ignored by the Japs, who must have considered it too unseaworthy to be useful to anyone. No one seemed to be watching it, and I decided that for the time being I would leave it where it was. When I had to begin actual work on it, I could move it to a less exposed place.

It wasn't until the end of May that I met William Desbres and Dirk Voorneveld. During all those weeks I had been busy laying in my supplies of food, working on the sail, and trying to find some of the other equipment needed for the voyage. I had made some headway on my own, but the time had come when I needed help. William and Dirk came into my life just as I was beginning to think there was no one in Java whom I could trust with my plans.

I had been invited to a Sunday evening party and the moment I entered the house I heard a man's voice telling my hostess that he was establishing a *prahu* company and was in Batavia looking for some boats to operate with. Immediately I had a feeling that this man was the one I had been waiting for. His story of a *prahu* company sounded suspicious to me. He didn't look as though he was the kind of man who would be content to manage a fleet of native *prahus*. I was introduced to William Desbres and his friend, Dirk, and spent the evening listening to their ideas. The more they talked the more convinced I became that these two had other fish to fry than those they might catch from the sea.

William was just my age, a tall, dynamic sort of person, full of restless energy and evidently afraid of nothing. Dirk was a few years older, a quieter, less forceful personality. Both men were from Bandung where they were now living a hit-or-miss existence under the Japs.

I said nothing of my own plans at the party. I listened to William talk and the more he talked the more sure I was that he was the man I needed. Dirk was his partner in the "*prahu* company," so he was of course to be included in any plans William and I concocted. I left the party with William and Dirk and once outside said quietly:

"Look here, about this *prahu* company—"

"*Prahu* company, hell," exclaimed William. "That's just a stall. I'm here to find a boat to get me out of Java."

That was all I needed to know. I immediately told them that I had found a boat, that I had collected a store of food and made some headway in outfitting the ketch. They listened enthusiastically and were with me at once. When William pulled a revolver out of his pocket and showed it to me, I was more than ever certain that he was the kind of person who would risk anything to get away. He had stolen the gun from the Japs somehow and told me that he had four more hidden in Bandung. Anyone who would dare steal five revolvers from the Japs was the man for me.

Of course, they wanted to see the ketch at once, so I agreed to take them down to the fishing harbor that very night. All of us felt tremendously elated as we bicycled down to the harbor. We discussed a multitude of plans, revolved schemes for getting hold of the instruments and supplies we needed and, in short, built a variety of castles in the air which were to whisk us away from Java in record time. There was a bright moon shining and its light acted like a charm on our spirits. We forgot all the mountainous difficulties that still stood in our path, for now that

Netherlands Information Bureau

THE THREE YOUNG DUTCHMEN AFTER THEIR 3000-MILE TRIP TO RODRIGUEZ

Netherlands Information Bureau

THE TWENTY-FIVE-FOOT FISHING BOAT AFTER IT REACHED RODRIGUEZ

Netherlands Information Bureau

INDONESIAN FISHING BOATS AT BATAVIA

Netherlands Information Bureau

A BRIDGE IN A JAVANESE VILLAGE

Malcolm Rosholt

A Japanese barber shop in Java

Netherlands Information Bureau

A STREET SCENE IN BATAVIA

Pony "taxis" at the railroad station in Batavia

A MARKET SCENE IN JAVA

we were in this thing together, we felt that nothing could stop us.

When we reached the harbor, I led them cautiously across the dock, keeping a sharp watch on the lookout tower for any spying Jap sentry. But no one saw us. Then I pointed dramatically to the spot where the ketch lay. My hand dropped to my side. The moon was reflected on the water in a brilliant glow that made it look like a sheet of gold. But the water was empty. The ketch was gone.

CHAPTER TEN

IT took me three days of careful reconnoitering to find the ketch again. I finally saw it moored just around the corner from its original position in a drydock that had once been owned by a Chinese. Now the Japs had control of the dock and three sentries patrolled it night and day. The boat lay right before my eyes, but now it was as far out of my reach as though it had never existed. I knew that there wasn't the slightest hope of getting it away from that dock. The sentries were too near and it would have been foolhardy to make any attempt to snatch it from under their very noses.

William was all for making a bold dash and grabbing the boat without a second thought as to where we could hide it, if we did succeed in getting it. I had some difficulty in persuading him that such a plan was utterly ridiculous. But he was too disappointed to be able to think clearly and kept on insisting that we could do it. When I had calmed him down, I made him see that we should have to begin all over again; find another boat and start from scratch with our plans.

Then Dirk had an idea. He and William knew somebody near Cheribon who owned a schooner which he kept at another harbor. They had already talked over the idea of escaping with this man and he had agreed to find out whether or not his boat had been scuttled by the Japs.

I didn't put too much faith in this scheme, for what they told me of their friend made me think that he wasn't any too anxious to get away. The Japs had been in Java for three months and if he hadn't found out whether or not his boat still existed in all that time, he couldn't be very up and coming. But any working plan was better than none, so I told William and Dirk to see what they could do with this fellow.

We decided that they were to go back to Cheribon immediately and talk to the man. The next weekend I was to come there and see if they had succeeded in getting anything definite out of him. I still had my job at the office, of course, and couldn't move about as freely as I would have liked. So I had to do most of my work on our plans in the late afternoon and on weekends. The Japs had issued strict orders that anyone caught taking time off when not necessary, slowing up on the job, or in any way acting suspiciously was to be heavily punished. I didn't want to spoil my chances by getting in wrong with the Japs, so I had to move carefully.

All that week I waited impatiently for word from William. He had promised to write me a postcard, giving some cryptic message which would tell me what progress he was making. But as the days passed and no card came, I began to get rather nervous. I wondered if I had been wise to tell the two men so much about my plans. I knew nothing of them really. They might even be Jap spies, though I thought this highly unlikely. Then, too, in spite of the confidence I had first felt in William's courage and self-confidence, neither he nor Dirk had ever done any sailing. They knew nothing whatsoever about a boat, and the responsibility of the coming voyage would fall entirely on my shoulders. I had chosen the two men to confide in because I liked their spirit. They obviously had strength of mind enough to make plans for getting away; they could help me enormously in the preliminary preparations. But once at sea, it would be up to me to get us across the Indian Ocean.

I had just about decided I had acted like a fool to tell so much to utter strangers, when a card came from William written in Malayan. "Johnny is well and hopes to see you soon," it said. From this, I knew that he had spoken to his man and that he wanted me to come to Cheribon to talk to him myself.

On Saturday I set out by train. I didn't feel any too happy about this trip, for stories had been circulating in Batavia to the effect that all trains were searched by the Japs and European men taken out and imprisoned. But I had to take risks to get what I wanted, so I tried not to think too much about what might happen to me if the train were searched. Like most of the rumors I had been hearing lately, this one proved to be false, at least as far as I was concerned. Except for a few soldiers traveling on the train, I saw no Japs at all. I merely showed my registration card when I bought my ticket, and when I reached the railroad station at Cheribon, the guards let me pass without so much as a second look in my direction. For the thousandth time I blessed that Kempei armband I wore.

William and Dirk were at the station to meet me and seemed in high spirits. They had made an appointment with their friend and we were to see him right away. I tried to find out what they had heard about this man's boat, but they were pretty vague on that score.

"Wait until we see ——," they said. And I had to be content with that, though my opinion of their friend began to sink away to nothing.

Almost as soon as we arrived at the man's house, I knew that I had been right in suspecting that he wasn't the sort of person who could help us at all. He was a businessman, a European who had lived in Java for years and was evidently quite wealthy. His life apparently had not been much disturbed by the Jap occupation and he and his family seemed very comfortably off. For two hours I had to listen to him discourse on his life and career. He described his schooner in minute detail and told us what a perfect boat it would be for our purpose. His desire to escape from Java was nothing but a dream of adventure to him and I soon saw that he had no real intention of leaving. He just liked to talk about it. He had made no efforts, even yet, to find out what had happened to his boat and this alone was enough to convince me that I was wasting my time.

"Look here," I said finally, cutting in on one of his interminable tales about his own prowess as a yachtsman, "what about your boat? Does it still exist or not?"

"Well—" he began, but I interrupted again.

"I'm going back to Batavia," I announced. "By next Saturday I want to know if your boat is still seaworthy. If not I'll get another."

He must have seen that I was beginning to lose patience with him, for he immediately promised to send someone down the next day to find out about his boat. With this I had to be content, but, when I left his house, I crossed him off my list of hopes. Boat or no boat, he wasn't going to be a member of our ship's company.

I went back to Batavia that afternoon, after arranging with William and Dirk that they were to follow me the next Saturday, bringing news of the man's boat and also all the personal possessions they would need for the trip. I told them to make their luggage light as there would be little storage space, whatever kind of boat we might find. The two men were to stay in Batavia until we left, since there was much they could do to help get ready for the voyage.

All that week I looked for a boat with no success whatsoever. That ketch seemed to be the only sailing vessel the Japs hadn't scuttled. But I wouldn't let myself get discouraged and continued to collect food supplies and other equipment just as though I had a boat all set for the voyage. Two native boys helped me buy the food. I sent them into the black market to get a little at a time, for I knew that I couldn't buy it all myself without rousing suspicion. Gradually the food stock at my house grew until I had fifty kilos of rice, forty-seven cans of corned beef, five cans of sardines, four cans of fruit, a can of sauerkraut, and two cans of prunes. It was a miracle that I was able to get so much canned stuff considering how strictly it was rationed.

I was still on the lookout for a chronometer and the necessary sea charts, but as yet had no luck in finding them. I wished William and Dirk would hurry and get to Batavia so they could help me. William, I knew, had many contacts there, and he told me of one man in particular who had worked with one of the steamship companies who might be able to help us in getting some charts. The only piece of real good fortune I had that week was running into an old friend of mine who must have had some idea of what I was planning, for, to my complete surprise, he told me that if ever I wanted any sailing equipment, I was free to use any he had. He had salvaged the sails from an old boat which he had sold and now had them hidden at his house. Without committing myself, I told him I'd remember his promise. The realization that I had this store of sailing equipment to fall back on gave my spirits a big lift.

It wasn't until Tuesday of the following week that William and Dirk finally showed up in Batavia. But I forgave their late arrival when I heard what they had brought with them. They had the five revolvers and some ammunition sewn up in a big piece of canvas, a case containing two gallons of gasoline, and a variety of small hand tools, such as a screw driver, a hammer, and some nails.

"But where is this stuff?" I asked, when William had finished telling me all about it.

"Oh," he said casually, "it didn't come on the same train we did. The baggage car was full, so it's coming on a later train. I'll have to go down to the station and get it to-morrow."

I groaned aloud, picturing what would happen to all of us if the Japs should happen to inspect the bundles, before William claimed them. But he reassured me by saying that he had sent them under an assumed name and planned to go to the baggage room and look over the stuff there before claiming his luggage. If he saw that his bundles had been tampered with, he was just going to walk away and do nothing about claiming them. He seemed so confident, I didn't say anything more, but I found myself praying that the Japs hadn't gotten curious about that bulky roll of canvas and the gasoline container.

They also told me that the man near Cheribon had found out that his ship had been scuttled and that there was no hope of using it. The man still talked of making a getaway, they told me, but I refused to listen to any more of his schemes. He wanted to get a native *prahu* and escape in that, but I knew enough about these fishing boats to realize that they'd never be good for a three-thousand-mile voyage.

As William had assured me, he had no difficulty at all in claiming his luggage at the station the next day. He hired a tricycle with a cart attached, one of the vehicles that were used in Batavia to transport goods. The natives did a thriving business with this "express" service, especially now when so many families were moving to cheaper quarters.

William made a careful inspection of the baggage room and soon discovered that his bundles were intact. The guard gave them to him without a murmur when he presented his claim check. It amused William to see the Jap hand him that canvas bundle containing the revolvers and ammunition. He packed the stuff in the tricycle's cart and led the way on his bicycle to my house, where we had agreed to keep all our stores. It was a load off my mind when I saw those bundles safely hidden in my cellar.

I explained to both of them what we still needed to outfit any boat we might find and stressed the fact that we must have charts of the Java Sea and a map of the ocean itself. We couldn't go anywhere without these. Charts of the Java Sea were particularly necessary as this part of our voyage might easily be the most dangerous, because of the reefs near the shore.

William is one of those people who are born lucky. He went the very next day to his friend from the steamship company and, without having to reveal our plans at all, got a lot of useful information for us, as well as some charts of the Java Sea. He also learned that the Japs kept a constant patrol of the Sunda Strait by planes and by boat. This news wasn't any too encouraging, but I had already decided that we would make the trip through the strait at night anyway and hoped to be able to avoid the Japs under cover of darkness.

We were making headway, but by the middle of June still hadn't found a boat. I began to get desperate. A native boy who worked in my office lived at Tanjung Priok and I tried to question him about the situation there. If some of the sentries had been moved away from the yacht basin, I thought I might have a slim chance of raising one of the scuttled yachts. But the boy seemed to know nothing of the Japs' activities and merely acted scared when I questioned him. However, I knew that the Jap sentries were always being changed; some of those at the Batavia end of the harbor had been removed entirely. Only those in the lookout tower remained.

The only thing to do was to make another trip to Tanjung Priok and look over the situation myself. I took William and Dirk with me late one afternoon and we bicycled the seven miles, talking rather dispiritedly about our chances of making an escape. We even discussed the possibility of buying a native *prahu* and trying to get away in that. This was William's idea and it took me some time to prove to him that, even if we had the money to buy a *prahu*, it would never be good for the trip we contemplated.

But the sentries were still thick at Tanjung Priok and we didn't even get off our bicycles to inspect the yacht basin. I knew that this seemingly last hope was blasted and that it was no good even to think of raising one of the yachts. We started back along the way we had come. Partly from habit I studied the masts rising above the roofs of the godowns along the riverfront. Perhaps I had overlooked the varnished mast I was hoping to see.

Then I saw it. Rising just a foot above the top of a tumble-down warehouse was the shining tip of a mast. Without inspecting it more closely I knew that it belonged to a European type of boat of some sort. The varnished mast proved that.

To the astonishment of William and Dirk, I said dramatically, "I've found our boat."

CHAPTER ELEVEN

THERE was no sentry in sight. We hid our bicycles behind a near-by building and ducked down to the wharf, moving cautiously in case we came upon a sentry by surprise. The boat lay at an obscure little dock, behind a native shipyard. It was a little twenty-five-foot cutter, with all the characteristics that made her a lively little sailboat. She had no bowsprit and a beam of eight feet. A small ship for a three-thousand-mile voyage, but I knew at once that she was the boat that was going to take us to Rodriguez.

"Hey!" William sounded frightened. "There's a sentry over there across the river."

He pointed toward a soldier who was patrolling on the opposite bank, evidently guarding the warehouses there.

"Never mind him," I answered grimly. "I'm going to inspect this boat. You fellows keep out of sight."

They protested, but I was determined to get a look at the cutter. I wanted to see what condition she was in and what we would have to do to outfit her for the voyage. The sentry looked in my direction, but made no move to challenge me. He watched me apathetically for a short time and then resumed his dreary beat.

I lost no time in giving the cutter a quick inspection. She had an open cockpit with only a two-and-a-half-foot freeboard, not a safe margin if we ran into heavy seas. Another point against her was the fact that the cockpit was not self-draining. In case of water coming in over that low freeboard, we would have one devil of a time pumping with the handpump. But I didn't give such drawbacks a second thought then. You can't expect to get just what you want when you're stealing a boat from under the noses of the Japs. There were plenty of good points in the boat's favor to offset those I could find fault with.

She was strongly built, copper riveted throughout with heavy teakwood ribs and planking. The bow and stern were the same, so she would stand a following sea well and a following sea was what we could expect to get. The cabin was small with only one berth, but there were possibilities of rigging up a second one. There were several lockers in the cabin and plenty of room in the bow to stow sails and other bulky stuff.

After noting these things, I began making a hasty calculation of what we would need to do to make her ready for the trip. All the stays were rusted away, the mast was in bad shape and the decks needed caulking. But these things could be done without too much trouble, though we would need help. William and Dirk didn't know anything about a boat and I wouldn't be able to get away from the office for long enough periods to get the job done quickly. I remembered the two native boys who had helped me in buying my food supplies and felt better. Both of them had some experience in painting and I knew they would be able to do what had to be done under my instruction.

"Hey!" It was William's voice again. "There's a native boy here who says he's in charge of this boat."

I left the boat and joined William and Dirk on the dock

where they were keeping out of sight of the sentry on the opposite shore. They were talking to a small Indonesian, who seemed pretty excited to find someone meddling with the cutter.

"This ship belong to *tuan* who live in city," he announced.

The boy explained, after my questioning him for some time, that the Chinese *tuan* who had hired him to watch the boat was an employee of the original owner. When I asked him if this man had the sails, boom, and rigging for the cutter, the boy didn't know. He just shrugged his shoulders and acted scared.

"Look here," I said firmly, pointing to my Kempei armband." I need this boat in my work. I have permission from the Japanese government to take over the boat, so you needn't be afraid." I gave him some coppers to look out for the boat and he felt better. He seemed to believe my story. With the coppers to grease his palm I felt pretty sure he would do as I told him. He said that the *tuan* came down to the dock occasionally to see the boat, and I hoped he would come again soon. If this man had the sails and other rigging, much of our outfitting trouble would be over.

"How are we going to get the boat fixed up with that sentry watching us all the time?" asked Dirk, as we rode away.

I confessed that this had been worrying me, too. I only hoped that if he ever challenged us, he would respect my armband.

"We can't let him stop us," I said impatiently, for Dirk was rather prone to find difficulties. "The worst of this boat is its position. When we get it outfitted, we'll have to take it out to the main canal under that drawbridge. The lookout tower is right beside the bridge and that's going to be a ticklish business. Luckily the mast is a folding one, so we can lower it to get under the bridge and not run the risk of having to raise the drawbridge when we go through."

We found the cutter on a Wednesday in mid-June and it wasn't until the following Sunday that I was able to get in touch with the two native boys. When I told them that I wanted them to work on a boat for me, they refused pointblank. Though they had been out of a job for three months, they weren't any too anxious to work for me as they were scared of getting into trouble with the Japs. It was only when I told them I had permission to use the boat that I could get them reluctantly to agree. The idea of having a job helped some, for they had been having a tough time getting enough to eat in the past few weeks. But they still weren't any too keen about the work, and it took constant prodding to keep them on the job.

I had succeeded in getting some oakum to caulk the deck, though I still had to find most of the outfitting materials. But we had enough to start with at least. We were just getting to work when one of the boys nudged me and pointed to a man who was standing on the dock watching us. He was an elderly Chinese, and as soon as I saw him I knew I'd have no trouble with him about the boat. His first words confirmed my feeling.

"I hear that you are taking charge of the boat," he said, when I had joined him on the dock.

"Yes," I replied. "I am starting—"

But he waved my words aside with a smile. "I see, I see. You should be glad I've kept my eye on it, because the Japs would have gotten it long ago if I hadn't."

I thought he wanted to be paid for his trouble and told him I would be glad to give him anything he had spent in caring for the boat. But he wouldn't listen to my offer. Then I asked him the all-important question.

"Have you the sails, ropes, and boom in your possession?"

He nodded. "Yes. You can come and get them at the storehouse."

My heart gave a leap. If he really had these necessary things, most of our troubles would be over. We wouldn't have to waste weeks making a sail from the canvas we had and trying to buy rope and other equipment.

The man gave me the address and went away, after I had assured him that I would be there the next afternoon to get the stuff. William and Dirk arrived soon after he left and my story of the meeting with the old Chinese gentleman gave them a tremendous lift.

I made out a list of a few things we would need to repair the boat, tools, paint, and so forth, and sent William and Dirk in town to get them. They went separately, as we didn't want to rouse suspicion by a wholesale raid on the shops. Most of the things we got from Chinese merchants, who often had a good deal of merchandise hidden away in the back of their stores which they would sell to people they knew and trusted. Gradually we accumulated wire brushes to scrape the rust from the mast, some lead paint and heavy scrapers to get the barnacles off the bottom of the cutter.

I stayed with the boat to show the boys what to do and got them started scraping the rust off the mast and barnacles from the bottom. By evening they had finished caulking the deck and begun the paint job. When darkness came, I had every reason to feel satisfied with the progress we had made. The sentry was still at his post and had been watching us all day. Either he was extraordinarily stupid or was pleased to have something to divert him, for he never so much as hailed us to ask what was going on.

The next afternoon, after work, I went to the storehouse as I had promised. I found some rope blocks, turnbuckles, a boom, and one mainsail stowed in a small godown. Still without questioning me as to why I wanted all these things, the Chinese gentleman gave me all the equipment without a murmur. I loaded it on a tricycle I had hired and, as soon as darkness fell, got it all transported to my house. I felt pretty nervous when I saw the telltale tricycle wheeling along ahead of me as I followed after it on my bicycle, for if any Jap sentry had wanted to stop me, I would have had some difficulty in explaining what I was doing with all this sailing stuff. I know that some people, the old Chinese gentleman among them, probably knew all along what I planned to do. But no sentries appeared and I got the things home without any danger, except to my nerves.

The Chinese gentleman had told me, when I saw that he had only the mainsail, which fortunately was in pretty good condition, where the rest of the sails probably were. I got the address from him and decided to try to get the jib and any other spare sails without delay. I took William with me when we went to the house the next day. We learned from the boy who welcomed us that the man who lived there had been interned and that his sister looked after the house. We asked whether she could see us.

As soon as we met the sister, I had a feeling that it wasn't going to be any too easy to get the sails from her. She looked rather suspiciously at us and was obviously a woman who had been through too much to put faith in any story we might tell her. After introducing ourselves, I made William, who is good looking and has a way with him, start the conversation by nudging him in the ribs.

"We understand that your brother has the sails of the boat lying in the fishing harbor," he began.

"Yes," was her brief reply.

"We are starting a fishing company," he lied, "and, since we are using this boat, will you kindly let us have the sails?"

"Well," she said hesitantly, "I can't decide that. I would have to get my brother's consent, but I'm afraid there's no way of getting in touch with him."

I saw that we weren't getting anywhere this way, for it was hopeless to suppose we could get her brother's permission. I decided to take rather strong measures and said boldly:

"The Japanese government has authorized our plans. We were going to send a couple of Jap soldiers to get the sails, but we thought it would be pleasanter for you if we came ourselves."

I felt pretty rotten to have to talk this way, but I wanted those sails and I knew we'd never get them except by bluffing her. The idea of Jap soldiers coming to the house horrified her and made her angry at the same time.

"Well," she said hastily, "if that's the case, you can have them." She went out of the room, leaving me feeling like a heel. After the war, I thought, I'll tell her the truth and maybe she'll forgive us for acting like this. After all, I told myself, the boat isn't doing her any good and it's a life saver to us.

She came back in a few minutes with a big bundle of sail in her arms and dumped it down at our feet. "There," she exclaimed, "take it and don't you dare send any Jap soldiers."

We thanked her profusely and gathered up the sail. When we left the house, she refused to say good-by to us and we heard her locking the door as soon as we were outside. But we were too elated at having the sails to give much thought to her justifiable anger.

When we got home, we inspected our new possessions and found that they consisted of three jibs, one of them quite new, a spinnaker and a balloon jib, both in middling good condition. All of them would need mending, but I knew I could do that easily. Now with the mainsail we had gotten from the old Chinese gentleman and the extra canvas we already had and from which I could manufacture some extra sails, we felt pretty well outfitted with sail. I remembered my friend who had promised to give me any of his equipment that I might need and went to see him. He gave me an old mainsail, much too big for the cutter, but it could be cut down if we needed it. I wanted to get as much spare canvas as possible, as most of what we had wasn't in first-class condition. A heavy wind might easily tear any of the sails to ribbons and I would need plenty of extra canvas to work with.

While the native boys worked on the boat, all three of us were kept busy trying to collect the rest of the necessary equipment. I tried to buy sail needles but there weren't any to be had, and I was forced to content myself with twenty of the biggest darning needles I could find. Sail thread was another thing we couldn't get, so we bought ordinary heavy cord. I didn't look forward to mending and making sail with these, but they would have to do.

I remembered a fifty-gallon tank which had once been used on a camp trip. I had given this tank to one of the native boys, before the Japs came, telling him that he might find it useful in case the city water supply was shut off. He had installed it in his backyard and now I told him to bring it to the dock. It arrived one evening and we had some difficulty in getting it through the hatchway. Once inside it filled half the available space, but water was the prime requisite of the trip and we didn't mind sacrificing comfort for a sure water supply. We braced the tank with wooden blocks, so that it wouldn't move when the boat heeled.

We were making progress, but there were still plenty of things we must have before we could think of leaving. Among these necessities were a chronometer, sea charts, and an almanac. Even more important was wire for the stays. There wasn't a foot of wire to be bought in Batavia. It began to look as though we had gone through all this suspense, trouble, and danger for nothing. Without wire and the sea charts we might as well stay where we were.

CHAPTER TWELVE

WE couldn't get the chronometer without telling someone what we intended to do. William knew someone in Batavia who had once done a lot of sailing. He found out that he still had his chronometer, but the only way he could get him to give it to us was to tell him all our plans. I hated to have to do this, for I was still operating on the theory that the fewer people who knew what we were up to, the less danger we would encounter. But I needn't have worried about this man. He gave William the chronometer instantly when he knew we wanted to escape from Java.

It was an old one and in pretty bad shape, but I was too glad to have it to complain about its deficiencies. The Japs transmitted a time signal from the Batavia radio station every night and I checked the chronometer with the signal. It showed an error of six and a half seconds every twenty-four hours and, knowing this, I felt I could correct my calculations from it.

I had the sextant I had bought from the Chinaman, but this too was an old instrument. William, who walked around in town almost every day, had the luck to find a newer and better one. We decided to take this along instead of the one I had.

The man who had formerly worked with a steamship company got some idea of what we were up to when William asked him for maps. For some reason he never suspected that I was going along on the trip and, knowing that William knew nothing about navigation, he questioned him as to who was going to navigate the boat.

"You're crazy if you don't take someone along who has a navigation ticket," he said.

"What kind of a ticket do you have?" asked William, who realized that the fellow was hinting that he be taken along.

"First mate," he replied promptly.

"Oh, well," said William airily, "we couldn't use you. You'd be parading the bridge too much."

The man looked pretty nonplused at this answer, but he must have seen that we had no intention of telling him anything more of our plans. He never again suggested we take him along, but he was good enough to help us. He found an old almanac for us, a 1938 one which was better than nothing, though it was four years out of date.

In an old book shop where we hunted for maps, we found two detailed charts of the Bay of Batavia, one which covered the area just off the shore near the city and another of the Sundra Strait region. There was a big gap between the two which left the area from the Thousand Islands to the mouth of the strait a blank.

Try as I might I couldn't find a chart for this section of the bay and I finally resigned myself to the fact that I would have to navigate it blind and trust to luck. If we ran into a coral reef—well, I wouldn't allow myself to think what might happen to us. Certainly it would mean the end of our voyage at the very least.

The chart of the Indian Ocean was harder to find, for they hadn't been as much used by yachtsmen as charts of the bay. We finally had to fall back on a publicity map. This was nothing more than a geography-book idea of the ocean with a scale of one inch to 238 miles. It showed nothing about prevailing winds or currents, and as a navigator's chart it was a dismal failure. But it was better than nothing and I was glad to have it.

A week had passed since we had found the boat. We had gradually gotten it into shape and collected most of the things we needed. It began to look as though we could plan on a day for our getaway. We hadn't dared store any of our supplies on board, for fear the Japs might seize it and take all the stuff we had so laboriously gotten together. All the food and instruments were still at my house and we intended to leave them there until the day we sailed. We worked out a careful schedule of how the boat was to be moved under the bridge and out to the outer canal. We weren't going to put any of the stuff aboard until the boat was in this canal, because it would have to pass the look-out tower to reach there and this was going to be the most ticklish part of the trip. If the sentries got too curious while we were moving the boat and inspected it, all they would find was an empty sailing ship.

The wire for the stays was still a problem. We couldn't buy any, for the Japs had confiscated every bit of wire rope in the city. I knew a man who was an electrician, and I thought it quite possible that he had a quantity of used wire in his office.

But he lived in one of the suburbs and all the way between his shop and my house I would have to run the risk of being caught. Moreover, I hesitated to go and see him because it was rather suspicious to ask for as much wire as I wanted. What could I tell him I needed it for?

But at last I had to take the chance and appeal to the electrician. I told him some crazy story about needing the wire for a chicken coop—a tale that I wouldn't have believed from anyone. He looked pretty doubtful, but at last he said I could have a few pieces if I would take it at night, so the Japs wouldn't see me. I selected some of the longest and strongest pieces and took them home after dark on my bicycle. I don't know what a sentry would have done if he had seen me. I wrapped the wire in old cloths, but it still made a suspicious-looking bundle. Fortunately, I didn't meet a single sentry between the shop and my house and got the wire safely stowed with the other things.

The next evening I took it down to the boat, still holding my breath for fear of being stopped, and showed the native boys how to rig it to the turnbuckles. Those turnbuckles had given us a lot of trouble. The original ones belonging to the boat were almost rusted away and I had only succeeded in getting two new ones. These I had fixed at the sides of the boat and had to be content with the old ones at the bow and stern. They weren't any too strong and I hated to think what might happen when any extra strain was put on them.

Now I could really see daylight ahead in our schemes. The boat was just about ready, as seaworthy as we could make it with the material at our disposal. The boys had done their work well, even though they were still scared the Japs wouldn't like it, if they found out they had been working on a boat. But we paid them well and a little money went a long way with them after their weeks of near starvation.

On a Wednesday I decided that we would leave the following Monday, July sixth. There were several reasons why Monday suited me best. It would give me Sunday for the multitude of last-minute preparations, and on Monday I would notify the office that I was sick. By the time the Japs came around to investigate my sick claim, I hoped to be far out of reach. It always took them a couple of days at least to look into such claims, and I was pretty sure they wouldn't show up until Tuesday.

Wednesday night a blow fell that almost knocked our whole scheme sky high. I was bicycling home from work when I noticed that there were an unusual number of sentries on the streets. It wasn't long before I found out what they were up to. One of them stopped me at a street corner and asked to see my registration card. I showed it to him and pointed to my armband, always a sure way of avoiding any difficulty.

"What's going on?" I asked in my halting Japanese.

"All European men between the ages of sixteen and sixty are being questioned," he replied with surprising good nature.

I didn't stop to wonder why he should bother to be so polite and communicative to me. In a flash I realized that William and Dirk were in danger. They had no Kempei armbands, no valid reason for being in Batavia. They were just the kind of people the Japs liked to get their hands on; young men who evidently had nothing to do and might be potentially dangerous to the Japs. As soon as I got my registration card back from the sentry, I headed for home as fast as I could make my bicycle go. I knew William and Dirk were waiting for me there and, if the sentries got to the house before I did, there was nothing I could do to save them. I saw, as I went along, that sentries were entering some of the houses on the street and my heart sank. Suppose they had already called at my house and picked up the unsuspecting pair.

I burst into the house at a run, deathly afraid that I was too late. To my overwhelming relief William and Dirk were lounging comfortably in the living room, quite unconscious of their danger. They looked up at my wild entrance in unconcealed amazement.

"What the—" began William, but I cut him short.

"Get into the kitchen both of you," I yelled. "Don't ask questions," I went on, as William protested. "Tell you later."

They obeyed me, still looking as though they thought I had lost my mind, as well they might in view of my action. Once they were safely hidden in the darkened kitchen outside the house, I made a careful inspection of the backyard. I decided that if the Japs came into the house to search it, William and Dirk could hide in the bushes and eventually scale the fence between my house and that of my neighbor.

William and Dirk didn't like the idea of hiding out. But when I drummed it into them that it was their one chance of avoiding the Japs and being able to make their escape from Java on Monday, they agreed to do what I told them.

We didn't have long to wait for the sentries. We heard a loud knocking and banging at the door. Only waiting to see William and Dirk's heels disappearing into the bushes, I went to open it. But the Japs had entered the house without being invited and were already searching the front rooms by the time I reached the door. They questioned me and once more I produced my registration card and showed them the armband. The armband had its usual magic effect and, after going through the rooms to see if there was anyone else in the house, they left. I had made no protest to their search and my apparent goodwill must have had some effect on them. They asked me if I was living alone and were quite ready to believe me when I said I was.

Ten minutes after they had gone, William and Dirk appeared in the kitchen. They were furious to think they would have to spend the rest of their time in Batavia hiding out, but I made them see that it was absolutely necessary. Now all the last-minute work of getting ready to sail must fall on me. But the greater part of it had been done, and in one way it was better for me to work alone with the native boys. Too many white men helping to move the boat would create more suspicion than one and two native boys.

That evening when I went down to the dock to tell the boys when I planned to move the boat, I found to my amazement that the sentry across the river had been removed. Why this happened I'll never know. But the Japs were always shifting their sentries and evidently this one was felt to be more useful elsewhere. There was no one sent to replace him, so for our purposes the Japs couldn't have chosen a better time to get rid of one of the biggest stumbling blocks to my plans. I had been wondering what the sentry would do when he saw us move the boat, but now I needn't worry any longer. It almost seemed as though the Japs were playing into our hands.

I told the boys that on Sunday night, right after dark, I wanted them to take the boat out under the bridge, past the lookout tower and around to the opposite side of the fishing wharves. These wharves were between the tower and the dock where I planned to moor the boat, so that the sentries could not see it during the daylight hours on Monday. Then Monday evening, as soon as it was dark, I told them to move the boat again, this time across the canal to a dock that connected with the highway leading from Batavia. We had to make this second move, as we were to load the boat just before leaving and we couldn't do this at the fishing wharf without taking a lot of unnecessary trouble and risk.

The last few days seemed endless. I couldn't concentrate on my work at the office and spent most of my time going over and over in my mind all that I must do on Sunday and Monday. Now that our plans were so near fulfillment, they began to look perfectly insane. How could we expect to get away with it? I asked myself over and over again. There were a thousand risks to be taken, a thousand chances of failure. Any small slip-up in our time schedule, an unlucky questioning by a sentry, or another search made at my house might easily blast our hope of escaping.

CHAPTER THIRTEEN

BUT Sunday, July fifth, came and nothing had happened to spoil our carefully thought-out plans. William and Dirk were still confined to my house; unwilling prisoners who felt themselves badly used to have to spend their last days ashore cooped up indoors. I kept them busy packing our stores and making compact bundles of all that we were to take with us. It was going to be a tight squeeze to stow all that we had in the cabin and still have room to move about. We cut our personal luggage to a minimum, and I left most of my possessions behind me.

Late Sunday afternoon, just as the sun was beginning to set, I bicycled down to the wharf to superintend moving the boat. The two native boys were already there, for they had spent the day doing some last-minute chores about the cutter. She didn't look any too trim with her makeshift rigging and worn ropes, but I was in no position to criticize. This boat, with God's help, was going to take us across the Indian Ocean and it wouldn't do to find fault with her.

A captain of a fishing *prahu* was sitting on the dock when I arrived, watching the boys as they lowered the mast so that we could get the boat under the bridge. He was chewing betel nut, spitting into the water and offering them the benefit of his free advice.

"Where are you going in that boat?" he asked me in Malayan, when he learned that the cutter belonged to me.

"Nowhere," I replied, but apparently he did not believe me.

The captain shrugged resignedly. "You will have trouble," he prophesied. "I have been sailing for years, but never until these dwarfs came have I had such trouble. A permit here, questioning there, rules, rules, rules. You can't make money and you haven't any freedom." He rambled along in this strain while I helped the boys with the mast.

"Look at that armband now," said the captain, spitting dangerously close to my feet. He gestured scornfully toward my Kempei brassard. "What does it say? Who knows that dwarf language? It's foolishness, all crazy."

I let him talk and even got him to help us. He was too interested in his own worries to wonder much about mine and I was quite content not to have him ask too many questions. When we finally got the mast folded, we began poling the boat away from the dock, for this was the only means of locomotion we had without sails. The last I saw of the captain, he had squatted down on his heels again, watching us as we disappeared into the evening dusk.

"Trouble, trouble. You'll have plenty trouble," I heard him muttering as we passed out of earshot.

But the old fellow was wrong, at least as far as this first leg of our trip was concerned. Before we reached the drawbridge, where we would come within sight of the lookout tower, I had the boys shove the boat near the bank, so I could jump ashore. I didn't want to run the risk of showing myself to the Jap sentries. A couple of natives poling an empty boat wouldn't rouse much suspicion. I hated to let the boys run the gauntlet of the lookout tower alone and they weren't any too anxious to expose themselves to the sentries either.

But it was the safest course and I urged them on by promising a fat bonus that would keep them in rice for weeks, if they got the cutter to the fishing wharf safely.

I watched them pass under the bridge and then turn to the right and head down the canal. This part of their trip was the most dangerous, for they would be in full sight of the sentries for at least five hundred yards, before they could swing to the left and get out of sight behind the fishing wharves.

I pedaled along beside the canal, trying to look innocent and apparently not paying any attention to the boat. From time to time I glanced up at the tower and through the windows could see the heads of the half-dozen sentries posted there. Once or twice one of them leaned out the window and stared apathetically at the scene below. But the boat must have seemed quite harmless to them, for, as far as I could judge, they never gave it a second thought. One of the sentries began to sing and the others took up the American jazz song, always a favorite type of tune with the Japs. I heard them laughing. By the time the cutter had made its turn to the left and disappeared behind the fishing wharf, the sentries were engaged in a cracked, high-voiced rendition of "Swanee River." For the moment the boat was safe.

Monday morning I sent my servant to the office with a note saying I was ill. This would explain my absence and I could only hope that the Japs wouldn't start their investigation of my sick claim that day. There were many people I should have liked to see again before I started, but I didn't dare for fear of their getting in trouble with the Japs after my escape was discovered. So I left Batavia, my home for twenty-two years, without saying farewell. I just disappeared.

Darkness came and with it the two native boys, who had already moved the boat again. I had hired a native cart to carry the bundles and we soon had it loaded with the food and sails. Now the real danger was beginning. If the cart were stopped and searched, there was no ready-made story to explain the food supply. The Japs would know something was up and there would be nothing I could say to make fifty kilos of rice and all those canned goods look innocent.

I went ahead on my bicycle and left the boys to follow with the cart. I hoped to be able to warn them of any potential danger, so that they could turn back in time. Our little cavalcade hadn't gone fifty yards before I saw that we were in for a bad time. The street was full of carts, carrying household effects, for, as I have said, many people were moving at this time and most of them did it at night when there was less bother from the sentries. But tonight dozens of extra sentries had been posted who were inspecting the carts, perhaps to see if they carried anything the Japs could use. My heart sank to my heels and I stopped where I was. Ten yards behind me the cart, too, halted. Should I turn back and wait for a more opportune moment or should I keep on? If we didn't get the stuff aboard that night and make our getaway, our whole scheme of escape might be ruined. We would have to hide the boat again and go through this whole procedure once more.

Then I noticed something that gave me a ray of hope. The sentries inspected most of the carts, but every once in a while, for no apparent reason, they let one go by without looking at its contents. Perhaps our cart would be one of the lucky ones. I decided to take the chance. Gesturing to the driver to follow me, I mounted my bicycle and went slowly forward. Not once did I look behind me to see whether the cart was still following. I didn't dare.

Holding my breath I went steadily forward. Past one group of sentries, past another that had stopped a cart. I didn't look at the sentries. My eyes were fixed straight ahead. It is over five miles from my house to the fishing wharf and I don't believe I took a deep breath the whole way. Once we were outside the thickly populated section of the city and in the business district, the sentries were not so thickly posted. I sneaked a glance behind me. The small, underfed horse was still ambling along, its head down and its weary feet plodding patiently on the pavement. The cart had not been stopped. I still didn't dare congratulate myself. We hadn't reached the boat yet and a hundred risks and dangers might lie in wait for us.

But we avoided them all. We passed three more sentries, all of whom merely stared at the tumble-down cart with its native passengers and the bulky bundles heaped inside it. The whole equipage looked too disreputable to be worthy of notice and the Japs let it pass unchallenged. By the time we reached the dock, our immediate troubles were over. Except for the sentries in the lookout tower, there wasn't a Jap in sight. It was too dark for these sentries to see what was going on below, and for the first time in what seemed hours I took a long, full breath.

Now that I look back on it, I realize what I was too busy to think much about at the time—the almost incredible luck we had in making our preparations for escape. Though we had many close calls, innumerable breath-taking moments, we never once were challenged by the Jap sentries while working on the boat. The nearest any of us came to a run-in with the police was a brief encounter between William and a native patrolman. Returning to the house one evening, he was stopped by a native who asked to see his registration card.

William hesitated a second to do some quick thinking. His card had been issued at Bandung and he knew that this fact alone would make the policeman wonder what he was doing so far from home. He made a pretense of searching in his pockets and then said carelessly:

"Must have left it at home. Come along and I'll show it to you there."

"You'll have to come to the station with me to report," replied the policeman, taking William by the arm.

"Rot!" exclaimed William, making a great show of annoyance. "I've been up to the station several times. They know all about me there. No use bothering with all that again."

The policeman, who didn't care to overwork himself for the Japs in any case, shrugged his shoulders and let go of William's arm. He probably didn't believe the bluff, but he was too apathetic about his job to make a point of it.

Before he could say anything more, William bid him good night and disappeared up the street at a fast clip.

That was our only direct challenge from either the police or sentries. It was luck that did the trick for us; without that blessing, we would still be in Batavia.

On that Monday night the darkness was also our salvation. Usually the area around the wharves is lighted by hundreds of kerosene lamps, the native means of illumination. But the Japs had confiscated all the kerosene and now the natives had to go without lights. We could hear them singing in the darkness as we quickly unloaded the bundles and stowed them aboard, heaping them into the cabin any which way. There was no time for orderly arrangement of our stores now. As they worked, the two native boys joined in the songs coming from the darkened houses surrounding the wharf. The mournful, dirge-like melodies made a dreary accompaniment to our work.

The boys had begun to get curious when they saw the stuff I was stowing aboard and their questions became pretty embarrassing. You wouldn't need all these food supplies for a trip to the islands in the bay, and it didn't take much intelligence to see that I had some other plan in mind. But money will cure most ills, even curiosity. The bonus I paid them, when the food and sails were safely aboard, was well spent. They realized they weren't to ask questions and the money shut them up like a charm.

Leaving them to guard the boat, I mounted my bicycle again for the final trip to town. When I returned, William, Dirk, and the rest of our supplies, the precious instruments and charts, would be with me and we would be ready to leave. On my way back to the house, I saw to my delighted amazement that the extra sentries had been withdrawn and now only the usual guards were posted at the street corners. I thought of the risks I had taken to get that first load down to the boat and what I might have avoided by waiting an hour or so. But the stuff was safely aboard, so I didn't waste any time in thinking about that first trip.

William and Dirk were wild with anxiety to get started

and had loaded themselves with all the equipment they could carry. Each of them had stowed a revolver under his shirt, leaving three more to be disposed of. They protested when I decided to stuff all three under my belt, but I wasn't going to let them out of my hands. I'd hired a tricycle to get this last load to the wharf and told William and Dirk to ride atop the load. Once the last of our stores was packed and William and Dirk were waiting in the tricycle, I took a last look about my house. There was no time for sentimentality. I just locked the front door and put the key in my pocket. Next time I came home—well, who could tell when that would be?

Once again I went ahead on my bicycle. Now it was well into the evening. Except for the sentries posted under the street lights, there was no·living soul in sight. I wondered what those Japs would do if they knew that the man riding past on a bicycle had three revolvers concealed under his belt. The revolvers were heavy and kept slipping down, so that I had to ride with one arm pressed close to my side to hold them in place. The sentries just stared at me. I saw one of them picking his teeth. Perhaps they were tired from their recent exertions in searching the carts. They looked utterly disinterested in me and in the tricycle following behind— a vehicle loaded with nautical instruments and carrying two men who had been in hiding for almost a week. What a catch those sentries would have made if they had felt inclined.

As we neared the business district, almost totally deserted after darkness fell, we passed the last sentry post. Two men were stationed here. I saw one of them gesture toward me and then at the tricycle. My hand crept toward the handle of one of my revolvers. If they stopped us, it meant our end.

I was going to take those sentries with me, if it came to a shooting match; take them wherever one goes when a bullet stops you. But the other sentry shrugged his shoulders and turned away. He wasn't going to bother and his companion didn't care enough about us to argue. They let us pass unchallenged.

We reached the wharf, safe at last in the darkness of the night. The native boys were waiting to help us throw the last of our stores aboard. The sails were set, everything ready at long last. I gave my bicycle to the boys.

"It's yours," I said. "Keep it for me until I come back." I jumped into the boat and grasped the helm. "Let her go," I directed William in a tense whisper. He untied the line and shoved the boat away from the wharf with both feet.

"*Slamat belayar, tuan, slamat belayar!*"

"Happy voyage, sir, happy voyage!" From the blackness of the wharf, already invisible behind us, the voices of the two boys followed us into the night. It was our farewell to Java.

CHAPTER FOURTEEN

A STIFF breeze on our port quarter pushed us out into the canal. The little cutter, glad to be released from its long idleness, seemed to skip over the water, drawing a long green trail of phosphorescent light behind her. Stretching out on either side of us were the long jetties which formed the entrance to the canal. The one at our right was submerged under the high tide waters; that to our left dimly visible in the gloom.

"Watch that jetty on the right," I cautioned, still speaking in a whisper. "We don't want to—"

"What's that!" William, crouched in the bow, sounded frightened.

"That" was a faint light playing fitfully at the end of the pier near the lighthouse. The big light was out, as it had been ever since the Japs came, but the flashlight told us that someone, probably a Jap sentry, was on duty at the end of the jetty.

"We'll duck out the side entrance," I decided, remembering with a rush of thankfulness the small opening in the sea wall to our left.

I was at the helm with both William and Dirk posted in the bow to warn me of obstacles in the darkness ahead. It was a piece of luck that I found the opening in the wall on the first try. We slipped through it and out into the bay.

"Fifty per cent of our troubles are over," I announced

somewhat dramatically. "We've only got the sea to fight now."

William and Dirk groaned in unison. "Only the sea," said Dirk mockingly. To them the sea with all its unknown terrors was as great a danger as anything we had been through ashore. But I knew something about the sea and felt more confidence than they.

"What about the Jap patrol in the strait?" asked William. "That's not going to be any picnic."

"We'll run the strait at night," I told them. "By morning, with this wind, we ought to be at the north end of the strait. We'll drop anchor and—"

"Good God, look out!" This time William fairly screamed the warning.

My heart jumped and I jammed the helm over to avoid whatever it was that William saw ahead. Not fifty yards before us were several dark shapes looming huge and menacing on the oily blackness of the water. I recognized them at once and began to laugh shakily.

"They're *prahus* lying at anchor," I explained to the indignant William. "We'll give them a wide berth." I swung to starboard and passed the motionless *prahus* without rousing the sleeping natives aboard.

I headed away from the shore out toward the open bay. Even here I knew we were running a tremendous risk, for coral reefs and tiny islands dotted the bay like plums in a pudding. Just north of us were the Thousand Islands, countless miniature landmarks, each one spelling possible ruin to our boat. The wind had shifted south, a brief spanking breeze that carried us along at a clip which would take us direct to the mouth of the strait, but at a speed that would stove in the hull, if we should strike a hidden shoal. I reefed the mainsail, the only canvas we carried aloft at the moment, and prayed for luck.

"Dirk!" I cried suddenly. "Come here and take the helm. William, you stay on watch and yell the minute you see anything ahead. I want to go below and take a look at the chart."

Dirk came back and I set the helm for him. In the cabin I grabbed a flashlight and directed its beam for an instant on the chart. In that quick glance I saw that we would soon be out of the area showing on this chart and into the unknown portion of the bay for which I had no chart. I snapped off the light. There was no use worrying. We'd just have to go ahead and trust to luck to get us through.

Once again on deck I peered forward. Directly in our path was the long low outline of an island. Why hadn't William seen it?

"What's the matter with your eyes?" I shouted, grabbing the helm from the frightened Dirk. "Don't you see that island?"

My eyes, more accustomed to the darkness and knowing what to look for on the sea, had spotted the vague shape which was not at all apparent to William. We swung around the small island, missing it by a bare ten feet, while William, too chagrined to make an answer for once, sat glumly in the bow.

"You'll get used to spotting them," I consoled him, feeling better now that the danger was past. "But keep your eyes open."

Thoroughly alert now, William and Dirk, who had once again joined him at the bow, redoubled their efforts and soon were as quick as I to spot the looming shapes on our path.

Their warning cries gave me an ample margin of safety and we avoided them all.

The prevailing wind in the Java Sea is generally south at night, shifting to the north during the day. I knew we could expect the favorable south wind until daylight and by that time I hoped to have covered the sixty miles from Batavia to the mouth of the strait.

No one thought of getting any rest that night. Except for an occasional trip below to flash my light for an instant on the charts, hoping to find that we had passed through the area which neither of my Java Sea maps showed, I stayed at the helm all night. We didn't talk much. We were too tense even to think. At any minute we expected a Jap patrol boat to show up or to find ourselves rammed against a hidden reef, powerless to move. None of us had thought of getting any supper before we left, but we weren't hungry even now. You can go without food and nourish yourself on anxiety indefinitely, if you have to.

Occasionally one of the reefs or shoals showed a light. All of them had been marked before the Japs came, but under their rule, the buoys and lights had been neglected and only a few were working. But these few were a tremendous help and their tiny winking lights seemed to signal a message of hope to us.

A pale glow was showing in the eastern sky, when I made another trip to the cabin to look at the charts. I gave a long sigh of relief. In the faint early light I had noted our position in relation to the visible islands. Now I knew that we had passed safely through the uncharted area and were in the region marked on my chart of the Sunda Strait. We had made it, in spite of the darkness, all the countless reefs and shoals in our path. What kind fate had led us through this perilous passage, I didn't try to determine. Ahead was the strait, patrolled as we had been warned by Jap planes and ships. Our troubles weren't over yet.

We dropped anchor some fifteen miles north of the strait just as the sun burst up over the sea, flooding the waters of the bay in a red glow of light. Morning had come with a vengeance and we could depend no longer on the protecting darkness which had been our salvation on the first leg of our flight. For the next twelve hours we would be in full sight of any marauding Japs.

The wind veered around to the north soon after we anchored and the little cutter bobbed in the freshening breeze as though anxious to get under way once more. I stared out over the water and wondered if I dared risk making the run now. The area looked harmless enough. Just ahead of us were a dozen or so fishing *prahus*, some of them raising anchor to begin the day's work, others content to try their luck in a stationary position.

"Well?" It was William who asked the unspoken question. I knew what he meant, for he understood the significance of these fishing boats as well as I. They might be our salvation. Another sailboat, even a European-rigged one such as our cutter, might easily escape the notice of the Japs in the waters of the strait. I knew that we could expect to meet these *prahus* all along the way. They might protect us by their very numbers if we tried the run during the day.

"There's no point in hanging around here like a dead duck all day as long as those *prahus* are about," I said slowly. "It would be safer to wait for night, but we can't be sure of getting a favorable wind like this. I don't know about the current, so we can't count on it to help us, if the wind drops."

"We'll be visible from both shores if we run through now," said Dirk nervously. "The Japs might—"

"To hell with the Japs," said William energetically. "I'm for getting started. I don't like this sitting around."

I grinned. "Two against one. We'll get going. The strait is eight miles wide and we'll be visible from both shores all right, but we'll take a chance. We haven't seen a Jap yet."

We weighed anchor, hoisted the mainsail, and soon were scudding along before the wind at a lively pace. I took the helm and headed direct for the mouth of the strait, some fifteen miles ahead.

"Say, look at those wrecks," exclaimed Dirk, pointing off to starboard at a cluster of buoys attached to the masts and funnels of several sunken ships. "Bet those are what's left of the Java Sea battle."

I nodded. We were almost at the mouth of the strait and I knew that the great sea battle had been fought in this area. Those desolate masts, rising above the water, were mute testimony of the destruction of our ships and those of the enemy. But our ship was alive. It was taking us away from the defeat and ruin that these ships meant to Java. We were on our way to revenge a battle like this and I didn't waste time in mourning over the graveyard of our once gallant little fleet.

"Look here," I said, as two *prahus* loomed across our path, "you two get below and begin fixing up that cabin. It's a mess with all that stuff strewn around. See if you can rig another bunk on top of some of the luggage."

The two ducked down the hatch, just as we passed some thirty feet to starboard of one of the *prahus*. The men aboard

116]

her stood up to stare at me and I saw them gesticulating and talking among themselves. They were too curious about the cutter and I didn't want to rouse suspicion even among the native fishermen.

"Chuck me up one of those bath towels and that fisherman's hat," I shouted, suddenly getting an idea for disguising myself. The towel and hat came flying up through the hatchway and I hung the former around my shoulders and pulled the hat well down over my eyes. With the bright blue towel as a makeshift shirt like the colored ones worn by the fishermen and the hat, I hoped to make myself look like an innocent native, in spite of the telltale European rigging on our boat. The ruse seemed to work, for I was careful to give all the *prahus* a wide berth and kept my face sheltered under the hat brim.

With a strong wind at our backs we entered the mouth of the strait about nine in the morning. Here the native fishing boats were scattered thickly over the water, all of them a welcome sight. The more *prahus* there were, the less chance there was of a Jap patrol spotting us. So far I hadn't seen any sign of the Japs. There were no planes overhead and the only boats in sight were the ever-present *prahus*. It began to look as though we might make it.

A baby could have handled the helm the way the wind was favoring us, so I yelled down to William to relieve me. I wanted to make certain that our stores were stowed away in a shipshape manner and particularly to see that our instruments were given a dry place.

"Hey, when do we eat?" asked William, when he appeared on deck.

"Not until we get through the strait," I answered grimly.

"We can't risk taking time to set up that charcoal stove until we're out in the Indian Ocean where we'll be safe from the Japs."

William groaned as he took the towel and hat from me and grasped the helm.

"Grab yourself some biscuits and some of those tomatoes," I said, relenting as I saw his crestfallen look. "They'll hold you."

I handed him up the biscuits and fruit and took some myself. Dirk was feeling rather green around the gills, for the boat was heeling pretty much in the stiff wind. I made him sit on the hatchway to get some fresh air, while I finished making the cabin shipshape. The other two had fixed a second berth on top of a couple of seabags and a spare mainsail, but it didn't look any too comfortable. We were to discover that the man who drew this berth had to lie at an angle of about twenty degrees with a sharp wooden brace to prod him in the back every time he moved. I wrapped the instruments in canvas and lashed them to a small shelf over the bunk.

The wind kept up all day, shoving us along at a good clip. Still no Jap planes or ships appeared. I couldn't understand why they neglected the area, but I wasn't going to worry myself on that score. Their carelessness was our good luck. We passed several islands in the strait, most of them deserted except for lighthouses. By nightfall we were off the volcanic island of Krakatau, a good sixty miles from the mouth of the strait. If we kept this up, we'd be well out into the ocean by morning and safe from any possible Jap patrols.

But I knew too much about winds and the sea to cheer at our good fortune and it was well that I didn't. Krakatau was lying to starboard, just visible in the dimness of the setting sun. I was pointing it out to William and Dirk when I realized that the wind had fallen suddenly and was now nothing but a mere puff at our backs. I looked over the side of the boat and to my dismay saw that the current was carrying us back the way we had come at a rate of about three or four knots.

I stared out over the water and up at the sky. There wasn't a ripple on the sea or a cloud in the sky to give me hope of a breeze.

"If this keeps up," I said nervously, "the current will carry us back to the mouth of the strait by dawn."

William and Dirk didn't say anything. There wasn't anything to say. They peered over the edge of the boat at the running current, listening to the slapping noise of the water pushing against the prow.

By eight o'clock we couldn't see Krakatau any more and were some ten miles back on our course. I whistled, snapped my fingers and swore, ably seconded by William and Dirk. But the wind made no response. The air was as still as though we were in a vacuum. A slight swell rocked the boat in a sideways, bobbing motion, that soon sent William and Dirk to the bow, where they hung over the edge, groaning and cursing.

I was too worried to think their agony funny, as many seamen do the seasickness of a landlubber. For several hours I sat glumly at the helm with nothing to do but keep the bow set on our backward course. At midnight a sudden rain squall shot up behind us, bringing a temperamental wind that sent us forward once more. I was too thankful to mind the fact that I was quickly soaked to the skin, for the fitful wind was carrying us toward our goal. It died again after an hour, but soon another squall sent us on again. So by fits and starts we pushed on and before dawn of July eighth were opposite Krakatau once more.

William and Dirk had spent the hours from midnight recovering from their bouts of seasickness in the cabin, but a shout from me brought them on deck at sunrise. A light eastern breeze had sprung up with the sun, carrying us along at about three knots.

"At this rate we'll be well out in the Indian Ocean by nightfall," I told them. "The chances of the Japs spotting us then are absolutely nil."

"Japs or no Japs," said William, "let's eat."

CHAPTER FIFTEEN

WE set up the little charcoal stove on deck and heaped coals under the grate. The ten gallons of gasoline that William had brought from Bandung came in handy as a quick method of getting the fire alight. Soon we had a hot bed of coals and a small saucepan of rice simmering over the grate.

"Bust out a can of that corned beef," I suggested. "It's almost time to congratulate ourselves. By sundown we'll be out of sight of any Jap patrol."

"What makes you so sure of that?" asked Dirk, getting busy with the can opener. "Since we didn't see any in the strait, they may be hanging around to the south of us."

"What for?" I demanded. "They've seen to it that all the sailing ships have been scuttled in Java—that is," I added with a grin, "all but this one. They wouldn't have any need to patrol out of range of a *prahu*. No, you can count on our being safe once we get out in the ocean."

"Wonder what we'd do if we did sight a Jap ship or plane?" asked William thoughtfully. "What could we do to make the boat look harmless?"

"First thing I'd do," I replied instantly, "would be to lower sail and turn the bow toward shore. The Japs would think we were headed for Java and probably not bother us. Or they might think we were a derelict ship and leave us alone anyway."

We speculated on possible means of fooling the Japs, in

case we were spotted, but it was more of a conversational exercise than a serious problem. My confidence had given William and Dirk a greater sense of security and they began to feel better. The rice and corned beef, washed down with a little water, gave us a lift and we were in high spirits all that day. By late afternoon we had left the strait behind us and were well out in the Indian Ocean, still driven along by the light easterly breeze.

Now we must depend on the publicity map of the Indian Ocean, for we had gone beyond the area shown on the chart of the strait. Fortunately the map was fairly accurate, but it was no navigator's dream at that. I marked our position on the map, getting it quite accurately, as we were still within sight of Prince's Island, at the southern end of the strait. I planned to take a sight with the chronometer and sextant the next day, but for now that was not necessary.

We decided that we must limit ourselves to two meals a day, morning and evening, for our stores were none too plentiful. The water situation was even more ticklish. We had fifty gallons aboard and I had no real idea of how long it would take us to reach Rodriguez. With luck and a good wind, we might hit it in a couple of weeks, but if things went against us, it might take two or three times as long.

"We'll have to plan on using only a gallon of water a day for the three of us," I announced at suppertime. "It's going to be tough, but we don't dare allow ourselves any more than that."

"Lord, I hope it doesn't get any hotter," said Dirk, when he had digested the fact that this would allow each of us only a little more than a quart a day for cooking and drinking. "It's fit to broil an ox right now."

He was right about that. The tropical sun had beat down on us with terrific force all day, making the deck little better than a sizzling frying pan. Even now, with the sun sinking, it was desperately hot.

"Wait until the sun goes down and you'll be cold," I told them. I had sailed these tropic seas enough to know that the contrast between night and day often sets one shivering at night after suffering the agonies of the damned all day. They discovered the truth of my prophecy before long and, when darkness overtook us, we were glad to put on sweaters.

The wind still kept its leisurely easterly direction, but it was enough to keep us going when I crowded all the sail aloft. Much of this work I had to do alone, for neither William nor Dirk knew the first thing about a ship. They were willing and eager to learn and were useful in hauling rope and setting canvas. But the main responsibility was mine. I was willing to have it this way, for I was captain of the boat and the other two my crew, albeit an untrained one. Until I could trust them for even so much as handling the helm without my guidance, I had to be everywhere at once on the cutter.

I stayed on deck all night, telling the others to get some sleep in the cabin. The breeze held, but it was dishearteningly fitful and light. At 4 A. M. on the ninth, it died away entirely and we were left sitting on the sea in a dead calm. A heavy swell showed that there was plenty of wind in other parts of the ocean, but it didn't come near us. The southeasterly trade wind that I had been hoping to strike about now refused to blow and I began to think we weren't so lucky after all.

At sunrise we were still becalmed, bobbing and swaying

about in the swell like a cork. William and Dirk weren't any too comfortable in that swell, but a breakfast of rice and beef made them feel for a while that life was worth living. We weren't too well stocked with coal, so I worked out a plan which would make it necessary to light the fire only once a day.

"We'll cook enough rice to last us all day," I explained. "One hot meal a day is enough anyway and we can go on cold rations at night. Dirk, how would you like to be cook?"

There were several reasons why I suggested this to him, the principal one being that he was not as handy as William about the boat and couldn't seem to get the knack of raising or reefing sail with the speed that might be required if we got a strong blow. He was anxious to do his part, however, so I decided that he could handle the cooking and cabin work.

"Well, anyway," I said some time later, when we were still heaving up and down in the swell but not making any forward motion, "we got through the strait. Let's open a can of that fruit to celebrate."

I wanted to keep their spirits up at all costs and the fruit helped some. It tasted like ambrosia, after our diet of rice and corned beef. Work also helps morale, so I kept all of us busy that morning rigging a blanket to act as an awning over the cockpit. This would protect us from the sun and we needed something for shelter from its burning fire. By the time the awning was up, we were all dripping with sweat. We took turns going overside to cool off in the ocean, but the water was soupy warm under the midday sun. Once on deck again we were as hot as we had been before our swim.

By noon on the ninth we had drifted out of sight of land

and now there was nothing to be seen on our horizon but a heaving mass of rolling sea. It made William and Dirk pretty uncomfortable to view this monotonous seascape, even though it meant that we were out of all possible range of Jap patrols.

"What makes the boat roll so much?" asked Dirk, evidently wishing that his stomach didn't follow the ship's motions quite so accurately.

"Wait until we get a breeze," I told him. "You won't notice it so much. Guess I'll take a sight, so I can check our position from my last dead reckoning."

I set up the sextant on deck and, after a good deal of fiddling around, managed to get the angle of the sun in relation to the horizon. It's no joke to get a sight in a small boat that is heaving and rocking in a heavy swell, but I managed what I hoped was a fairly accurate reckoning. Our position was Latitude 6 44 40 S, Longitude 104 12 45 E. We were about a hundred miles from the north mouth of the strait where we had left the Java Sea and had covered forty miles that day. Not bad considering we had been becalmed for the past eight hours, but I hoped we'd average a better daily run in the future.

Shortly after noon a light easterly breeze sprang up again that carried us along at about two or three knots with all sails aloft. Later some rain squalls served the double purpose of cooling us off and speeding us up to about six knots. But the winds were squally and we were kept on the jump changing sails and trying to set them so as to get the most out of the chancey wind.

That night, after a cold supper, we arranged our watches. We planned to stand two-hour periods on duty and four off, when we hoped to get some sleep in the cabin. In case of bad weather we were to take one on and two off. I took the first watch at eight in the evening and sent the other two below for a rest.

All that day I had been instructing William and Dirk in the art of keeping the boat on its course and felt fairly confident that they could handle her, unless an unusual blow came up. But as it turned out, I seldom got much sleep during my periods off duty. William followed me at the helm at ten in the evening and I went below, tired as a dog. But I couldn't sleep. Every slap of a wave against the prow seemed to sound a warning, the rattle of the stays and creak of the ropes and sail all meant something to me. I lay on the bunk listening to the ship breathe, fearing every moment that something would go wrong.

I had impressed upon both William and Dirk the importance of never leaving the helm to go forward to shift sail.

"If you leave the helm, even for a second, without calling for someone to relieve you, you'll find yourselves in trouble," I said. "A wave or a lurch of the boat might knock you overboard and we'd never know you were gone. Don't forget that."

I'd drummed this into them so hard that they both kept a tight grip on the helm whenever they were on watch. They were so new at sailing that every time the canvas flapped, they'd sing out to me to come and tell them what to do. They still hadn't gotten the knack of keeping the ship close to the wind and when they were at the helm we didn't get as much out of the wind as we might have.

The wind was variable all night, never strong unless a rain squall shoved us along at about six knots. After midnight a heavy rain fell and we collected a couple of gallons from the water that dripped off the sails. By daybreak we'd refilled the tank again and began to feel that a water shortage wasn't going to be our big worry after all. It was the wind that really bothered me. I'd hoped to hit the southeast trades before now and here we were still being knocked around by nothing more than occasional rain squalls.

By daybreak on the tenth we were wallowing around in the same rolling sea, making little or no headway. The rain served one good purpose in cooling us off and not making us so thirsty, but I'd have sacrificed this advantage for a good stiff southeaster.

Dirk cooked some potatoes for breakfast in seawater, a culinary stroke of genius that saved our water and really improved their taste. We were all rather dispirited at our lack of progress, for it didn't take an experienced seaman to realize that we'd gotten just about nowhere in the past twenty-four hours. Our noon position showed Latitude 6 47 30 S, Longitude 103 28 15 E, a run of forty-eight miles since the previous reckoning. We'd have to do better than that or we'd be hanging around too near Java and the Japs for comfort.

Just after taking the sight the wind died away completely and we were at the mercy of the rolling swell. The ship was heaving up and down, back and forth like a rat in a terrier's mouth, and William and Dirk cursed the day they were born.

"Why in hell those rollers don't sweep over the boat instead of under it the way they do is a mystery to me," said William, staring apathetically at a green mountain of water towering above us. He watched it sink away under our keel and shook his head disbelievingly. It had looked as though it would break just over our heads and I couldn't blame him for wondering why it never did.

"What gets me is how the damn boat can rock so much and not turn over," said Dirk, who was clutching the freeboard with both hands. The little cutter spent much of its time at an angle of about forty-five degrees and to a landlubber it looked as though every lurch would be its last.

"Well, you can thank your stars she's as seaworthy as she is," I said defensively. "You keep your eyes open and watch everything I do and you'll learn all you need to know about this boat."

"All right, Captain Jenks," exclaimed William a moment later, "what is that rope doing flapping around the mast?" He was at the wheel when he spoke and I was lounging halfway up the companionway staring out over the stern and wishing I could see something that looked like a wind approaching.

I whirled around. One look was enough to show me that the mainsail halyard had broken. The rope hadn't been new when we started, but I had hoped it would last longer than this. I began to swear, while the other two laughed. The accident gave them a good chance to get back at my boasting.

"You won't laugh so hard when we pull you up that mast in a bos'n's chair," I told Dirk, as I went forward.

The only extra rope we had was larger than the broken halyard so I had to climb the mast to fit a bigger block at the top. It wasn't much fun shinning up the mast with the ship rolling and lurching like a drunken man. If I'd had an extra pair of hands, it might not have been so bad. But as it was I used about one and a half hands to keep myself steady and half a hand to do the necessary work. I felt like a flag on a pole swaying and bobbing around atop that mast and every minute I was certain that I'd lose my grip. It took me about five times as long to fit the new block as it would under ordinary circumstances. It was secure at last however, and William and I hauled Dirk, the lightest of the three, up in the bos'n's chair to run the new rope through the block. He didn't like his trip aloft one bit and looked pretty green when we finally lowered him to the deck again. It had been a risky business, but the new halyard was in place.

"Hadn't we ought to reef sail a little?" asked William, when we were once more established in the cockpit. "They're taking a hell of a beating from the swell and aren't getting us forward at all."

I'd already considered this point and had debated in my mind the advantage that might be gained from the fitful squally winds by keeping all sails set. Certainly they were taking a lot of punishment from the lurching rock and sway of the swell, but I decided that it was better to keep them up and try to make headway.

"The only thing that worries me is that they aren't any too strong," I explained. "We'll be patching sail before long, but I'd rather do that than sacrifice any wind we might get."

All that afternoon we were becalmed, at the mercy of an occasional rain squall which sent us forward for a few minutes and then left us to the rolling swell. To help pass the time, we got out the revolvers and practiced shooting at the sea snakes that rode the surface of the waves some distance from the boat. We weren't Annie Oakleys by any means, for we didn't hit a one. But the sport took our minds off our troubles and gave us something to do besides grouse at our hard luck. Just as we put the revolvers away a shark nosed up out of the water not twenty feet from the stern and gave us a mean going over with his piglike little eyes. We comforted ourselves for our previous bad shooting by thinking that we'd surely have gotten him if only our guns had been handy.

I had been heading the ship due southwest and west southwest in hopes of picking up the trade, but by the morning of the eleventh we were still just about where we had been the evening before. But we found something to occupy us, in spite of the lack of wind. As I had feared, the sails, none of them in first-class condition to begin with, began to show the effects of the pounding they were getting from the ship's uneven motion. Right after breakfast I reefed in the mainsail, for it was showing several spots that needed patching. I showed William and Dirk how to make a patch, but it wasn't easy work sewing with darning needles and cord on that unwieldy canvas. We had plenty of time to do the work, however, and by noon, still in a dead calm, we had the sails repaired.

I got the noon sight, Latitude 7 10 S, Longitude 103 20 E, showing a discouraging day's run of twenty-eight miles, just before the sky clouded over. The clouds brought the wind, however, and it began to look as though we had hit the southeast trades at last. Our spirits rose with the wind and by suppertime we were feeling fairly jubilant. We were hitting about six knots now and, if our luck held, we ought to average sixty miles per day.

At eleven that night I came on deck, though it wasn't my turn at the helm, just to see how William was getting along.

I found him staring out off our starboard quarter, looking as though he were seeing a whole troupe of ghosts.

"What's the matter?" I asked impatiently, for he was neglecting the ship entirely.

He pointed and, following the direction he indicated, I saw two huge ships, lighted up like Christmas trees, passing to windward.

IT seemed totally unreal to see these ships, lighted up as they were, in this warring world. As they came nearer I saw they were sailing parallel, evidently keeping close together for mutual protection.

"Let me have the helm," I shouted, grabbing it from William's hands. "Got to steer clear of them."

I tacked southward, keeping to windward about five miles. As we watched their blazing lights disappearing over the horizon, I wondered what would have happened if we had met those ships during the day. They couldn't have missed us and it would probably have meant the end of the voyage for us. To me it was just another evidence of the luck that had graced us so far.

"What are they?" asked William, staring at the glow of light that marked their position on the horizon. "What ships would sail this ocean all lighted up like that?"

I had been wondering this myself, but now I remembered something I had heard before leaving Java about an exchange of diplomatic representatives. "My guess is that they are American and British consular people being taken to Lourenço Marques in Portuguese East Africa. I heard that they were going to exchange them for Jap representatives there."

Later I learned that my guess had been right. But at the moment I didn't much care what the ships were as long as we had missed being sighted by them. I stayed on deck most of that night, for the wind was sending us along at a pretty good clip now and I liked the feeling of making progress. I couldn't sleep anyway and it was better to lounge on deck than toss around in the makeshift cabin bunk. William was kept on the jump by the porpoises which occasionally took it into their silly heads to surface just by the stern of the cutter, scaring him half to death. The showers of spray they threw over the cockpit kept him wringing wet and mad as a hatter.

By dawn we were still making good headway, about six knots I judged. It was a fine sunny day and flocks of seagulls appeared around us, attracted as they always are to a boat in hopes of finding food. They were disappointed in us. We didn't have enough to afford garbage, but the gulls hung around, squawking and shrilling overhead. Some of them tried to light on the gaff, but it moved too often for them to get a footing. Occasionally one would perch for an instant on the top of the mast, not a comfortable resting place, even for a gull who isn't very choosy.

"Let's take a shot at one of those damn birds," suggested William, who didn't care for the calling cards the gulls were leaving on the sails and deck.

"No, you don't," I replied quickly.

"Superstitious?" he asked grinning. " 'With my crossbow I shot the albatross' and all that?"

"Perhaps," I said. "Anyway I don't believe in killing a bird just for the fun of it. You can't eat seagull and I like to watch them anyway. It's amazing how ugly they are when they're sitting still, but once they spread their wings there's nothing more graceful."

"Hey," shouted Dirk from the cabin just at that moment, "the water tank's leaking!"

This was a catastrophe and I jumped down the companionway to see what could be done about it. The leak was in the tap and, after some fooling around, I rigged a rubber tube that we had brought along for no good reason and attached it to the top of the tank. The tap couldn't leak now and I wondered what streak of luck had made me take along the rubber tube.

Our noon position this day, July twelfth, was Latitude 8 25 10 S, Longitude 101 53 15 E, a day's run of 102 miles. We were in high spirits when I announced our progress and spent the rest of the day telling each other how clever we had been in making our getaway so easily. Now we knew we were too far out in the Indian Ocean to have any believable story to tell the Japs in the unlikely event of their patrolling the region. In the Sunda Strait we had fixed up a story, if we were stopped, to the effect that we were on our way to Pelabuan Ratu on the south coast of Java where we were joining a fishing fleet. When we left the strait and were just entering the Indian Ocean, we planned to say that we were on our way to Padang on the west coast of Sumatra to look for freight for a shipping company to be established in Batavia.

We had discussed these stories at the time in order to get them straight, but now that we were so far out in the Indian Ocean there was nothing to explain our presence there. There wasn't much likelihood of meeting a Jap patrol, so we weren't very worried about it. We hauled in the small Japanese flag we had been carrying on the masthead, glad to get rid of it, and tossed it overboard. Now we had no flag to identify ourselves by, but for the present at any rate there wasn't any necessity for one.

The wind held and by noon the next day we had covered 120 miles since the last sight. If this kept up we would reach Rodriguez sooner than I hoped. But I didn't dare do too much cheering and warned William and Dirk not to expect such luck every day. From our position on the map I saw that we were running pretty close to Cocos Island and shifted to a more westerly course. I had been told before leaving Java that the Japs had taken Keeling Island, or Cocos as it is usually called, and didn't want to risk running too close to enemy territory. I found out later that the Japs didn't have the island and we might have cut our trip by three-fourths. If I'd known the British still controlled Cocos we would have headed for it in the first place. I don't know how the false rumor got around that the Japs had taken it, but it was typical of all the stories that were floating around Batavia while I was there.

The afternoon of the thirteenth I rigged up the spinnaker to take advantage of the strong wind. But when Dirk was at the wheel that evening he got a little careless, probably because the pressure on the helm was so light, and let the mainsail jibe on him. I decided to forget the spinnaker after that. It was better to sacrifice the advantage it gave us, rather than trust the inexperience of my crew.

"Why don't you rig the jib again?" asked William, when he saw that I was letting the boat sail under the mainsail alone.

"It's too worn out to be worth anything," I told him.

"This wind will tear it to ribbons and we don't want to bother patching it. We'll get along all right with the mainsail, if this wind holds."

"Well, I wish it didn't throw up such a sea," said Dirk, trying to dodge a comber that came rolling along the deck. It put several inches of water into the cockpit and we began to use the handpump, all of us wishing for the thousandth time that we had a self-draining system to take this tiresome load off our hands.

We were soaked to the skin most of the time now, as our raincoats were absolutely worthless once they were wet. We missed oilskins, but it had been impossible to get any before we left. Dirk wondered why we didn't get pneumonia what with half baking by day and shivering at night, but he soon learned that you don't catch cold at sea. None of us so much as had a sniffle the whole time we were in the boat.

By the next morning we were well clear of Cocos Island and I set a straight course for Mauritius, a larger island just west of Rodriguez. We would strike Rodriguez first, but I made Mauritius our objective for purposes of navigation. My map showed it to be 3020 miles from Batavia, one hell of a long way from where we were now.

"Why don't we head for Diego Garcia?" asked William, who had been studying the map. "It's just west of us and about half the distance to Rodriguez." He indicated the tiny island lying about a thousand miles due west of our position.

"I thought of that," I explained, "before we left Batavia. There are several reasons why it isn't such a good idea. In the first place it's entirely surrounded by reefs and shoals and, without a chart of the area, we'd be fools to risk trying for a landing there. Then Diego Garcia is about as flat as a pancake and we could sail right by it in a heavy swell like this and never spot it at all. Rodriguez is mostly rocks and hills and we can't miss it once we get within sight of it."

"It's too near the Jap sea lanes, too, I suppose," said William, after studying its position more closely. "Right smack below Ceylon and the Japs are hanging around there like flies."

I nodded. "It's best to steer clear of any place the Japs have their eyes on. No, I think we'll be better off heading for Rodriguez. It'll take longer, but, if we keep up this speed, we'll make it all right."

All that night the ship rolled so heavily in the tremendous swells set up by the trade winds that none of us could stay in our bunks. We'd taken on so much spray that the decks began to leak, too, and a lot of water seeped down into the cabin. If we did try to sleep, a couple of drops of water would land on our faces and wake us up with a jerk. But we didn't mind any discomfort as long as we realized we were making such headway.

Cooking next morning was a gymnastic exercise. The boat was pitching and tossing so much that two of us had to hold the stove, the saucepan, and the coals in place to get the food cooked. It wasn't much of a meal when it was ready, but better than cold rations at least.

The mainsail began to show a tear near the mast later in the morning and I reefed it in a bit to keep it from growing bigger. We were pitching around too much to make patching a very easy job at the moment and besides we made plenty of headway, even with a reef in the sail. I put the jib back on again, however, in spite of its worn condition, to feed more wind on the mainsail. It wouldn't last long, but I thought we might get what good we could out of it before it tore itself to pieces in the wind.

Our noon position on the fourteenth showed Latitude 9 16 55 S, Longitude 97 39 30 E, a run of 145 miles. The best we'd done so far, but the wind would have carried us along even without a sail at the rate it was blowing. I began to wish it wouldn't blow quite so hard, an odd wish for a seaman, but, considering the condition of our sails, an understandable one. We carried some spare canvas and an extra mainsail, but it would have to be recut to fit our mast and I hoped that the one we had would last the voyage.

By the time my watch ended at ten that evening, the wind was roaring overhead like a herd of angry bulls. The sails were straining at their ropes, as though anxious to get away, and a soaking spray kept the cockpit half awash. Someone had to pump all the time to keep it from filling entirely. We were making good time and nothing serious had happened to make me feel anxious, but I was just the same.

"Watch her," I told Dirk, when he came up out of the cabin, rubbing his eyes and yawning. "Keep her headed into the wind and for God's sake don't let the mainsail jibe."

He seemed annoyed at my advice, as well he might have been, and I lingered for a time on deck to study the sky. It was beginning to cloud over a bit; dark masses were rolling up along the horizon and I wondered if the storm would hit us. William came on deck to help with the pumping and I decided to go below to try to snatch a little sleep. I'd been up most of the previous night and knew I was getting too tired to be as alert as I should be.

"Get along, grandma," said William laughing, as I went

down the companionway. "We'll watch the baby for you."

I didn't tell them that I was afraid we were in for a storm. No use to worry them and I would be on deck again before it hit us, if it was going to. I threw myself across the bunk and, in spite of a persistent trickle of water running down my neck from the deck above, fell into a deep sleep.

It was a crash and a wild yell from Dirk that wakened me. I was on deck before I was fully awake. What I saw there made me forget there was such a thing as sleep. The cutter was pitching wildly in a massive heaving sea, its mast broken short and lying off the starboard quarter in a soaking tangle of ropes, spars and sail. A great wave washed over us, almost filling the cockpit, and the boat swung helpless in the trough of the sea.

CHAPTER SEVENTEEN

"HEAD her into the wind!" I yelled to Dirk. Lunging forward, I grabbed the helm from him and shoved it hard over. But the drag of the mast and sails to starboard was too much for me. I couldn't keep the bow headed forward with that mass of tangled wreckage pulling us around to starboard. There was nothing to do but let the ship have her own way and ride in the trough of the waves like a lifeless hulk.

Seeing there was nothing to be gained by struggling with the helm, I lashed it and went to inspect the damage. A driving rain began to fall just then, the storm I had seen forming along the horizon a short time previously. At the moment we scarcely noticed it; we were too concerned with the tragedy that faced us.

No one had a word to say as I made a hasty inspection of the cause of the accident. A glance at the stub of the mast showed that it had snapped off about three feet above the deck, just over the hinge point. The wood was decayed there and, weakened by the wind of the last few days, had given way in the gathering storm. The two turnbuckles of the jib stays were ripped out by the mast's fall, so that every bit of canvas had gone overboard with the mainsail. We got the jib in, as it was floating in the water, practically undamaged.

But the mainsail was a sorry sight. It was wrapped tightly about the mast, held there by the tangled stays. These ropes and wires were still attached to the boat and were the only thing that kept us from losing the mast and sail entirely. The canvas was torn to shreds by the fall and the beating it was taking from the lashing waves. The boat was pitching and tossing so violently that I knew it was foolhardy to try to get our ruined sail aboard that night.

"Lend a hand with these ropes," I shouted, grasping a floating halyard. I braced myself against the freeboard and began to haul on the rope.

William and Dirk, balancing precariously in the heaving boat, did as I directed, and after a herculean struggle we got the mast lashed alongside, using the broken stays to do the work. Once the mast, wrapped in the shredded sail, was secure, we sat back in the cockpit to view our impossible situation with what calm we could muster.

Both William and Dirk were so utterly discouraged by the disaster that I saw I would have to assume a confidence I was far from feeling to keep their spirits up.

"We'll begin hauling the mast aboard in the morning," I announced, trying to sound as though the task were going to be easy.

"We better give up the whole damn trip," said Dirk, making a desperate clutch at the freeboard to save himself from falling overboard as the boat heeled. "We could row to Cocos from here."

"And let the Japs stow us in a concentration camp—or worse—for the rest of the war," I answered scornfully. "Not on your life. We aren't licked yet. Wait until morning and you'll see."

I didn't mention the fact that we were well over a hundred miles from Cocos, a long row, even if I had wanted to try it. I was determined not to show my own discouragement and for the rest of that night talked like a fool to keep up my own courage as well as theirs. I made them tell me their life stories and added mine, with many embellishments, just to have something to keep the conversation going. But never for a moment could any of us forget our real danger. The sea and wind saw to that. The storm was going full blast now and, if we had thought the boat heeled too much before, we felt as though we were in a swing now. It was only by hanging on with both hands that we kept from falling overboard. The rain pelted down and what with that and the heavy spray from the great rollers, the cockpit was half awash all the time. We had something to do in taking turns at the handpump. But it was a small one and we were never able to keep the cockpit free of water.

We were all glad when a faint light along the eastern horizon showed that the night was over. But the morning that finally came was not a cheerful one. Heavy clouds still covered the sky and not a beam of sunlight penetrated them. The rain kept on, but now we were so soaked that we paid little heed to it; it was merely another torment to add to our long list of troubles.

"How the devil are you going to get that mast aboard and what are you going to do with it if we do haul it in?" asked Dirk, staring at the snarled mass of wood and canvas which looked even more of a wreck in the gray light of day. "We haven't any tools to fix anything with."

"Oh, shut up," I shouted, tired of his Jonah attitude. "We've got a screwdriver and a knife, haven't we? Lend a hand here and don't talk so much."

It took us two hours of backbreaking work to get that

mast and mainsail aboard; work that wasn't helped any by the fact that we had to hang on to the pitching boat like grim death while we struggled with the bulky wreck. The sea had not quieted with daylight and the cutter was still tossing and wallowing like a derelict. We got it aboard at last, however, and a sorry sight it was. The mainsail was ruined beyond repair; there was scarcely a square foot that didn't show a hole or tear. There was no hope of repairing it. I'd have to fashion a new mainsail out of the spare one we carried, a job I didn't look forward to.

Just as we gave the mast a final haul to settle it on deck, the main boom snapped. It had never been in first-class condition and the extra strain had been too much for it.

"Well, that's dandy," I exclaimed, sitting back on my heels to survey the damage. "Broken mast, busted boom. What more could you want?"

"I say we row to Cocos," repeated Dirk stubbornly. "We can't do anything with this mess."

"And I say we can," I said with more spirit. "William, get the breadknife and the file from the cabin. I'm going to start cutting down the mast."

"And then what are you going to do with it?" asked Dirk sarcastically. "Hold it up in one hand all the way to Rodriguez?"

I kept my temper with an effort and began to explain what I intended to do. "I'll cut about three feet off the end with this knife and drill a hole in it with the screwdriver and hammer, so we can set it up at the hinge point. You two can get busy splicing rope. We'll have to splice almost all the stays and halyards before they can be used again."

I showed them how to splice and, using the screwdriver,

they took turns at the job. But it was slow work for inexperienced men. Their efforts were a good deal hampered by the fact that I made one of them stay at the helm all the time to try to keep the boat headed into the wind. The other had to take time off every fifteen minutes or so to work the hand-pump. The spray was still coming in constantly, and every so often the water had to be pumped out of the cockpit or we would soon have been swamped. Then, too, the boat never stopped rolling and plunging, no matter how successful the helmsman was in keeping her bow to the wind. This sickening motion affected all of us and made our work twice as difficult.

Four hours' work with the breadknife and another hour with the screwdriver and hammer gave us a new mast. It was a tedious business, for I had to sharpen the knife every five minutes on the file and more than once I wondered if I were foolish to try to fashion a mast by such a toilsome process. But it was the knife or nothing and I kept at it. I felt rewarded when I at last saw I had finished the job. Now setting it up would be another problem. We'd have to wait until the storm let up before trying this, as it was going to be hard enough getting the heavy, unwieldy mast on our shoulders without trying to balance ourselves in a rocking boat at the same time.

The other two had made some headway with the ropes, but I saw it would be some time before they were ready for use. I made them keep at it, however, while I got to work on the mainsail. The spare one we carried had originally been cut for a schooner and would have to be completely remade for the cutter, especially now that I had cut down the mast. The light darning needles and heavy thread didn't help me with the job, and by the end of the afternoon I had made discouraging progress.

We hadn't cooked any food that day, for we wouldn't have been able to keep the stove upright. At noon we'd each had a chocolate bar and when evening came another piece of candy served as our supper. What with little food and all the work and worry we had been through, we were dead tired long before nightfall.

"Let's turn in," said William. "We can't do anything more in the dark."

"We've got to rig a sea anchor before we quit," I told him. "I want to try to keep headed into the wind and a sea anchor may help."

I made a sketchy sea anchor out of a spare piece of canvas and attached it to a rope at the bow. Nothing happened. The boat still persisted in riding abeam of the waves in a sort of helpless "what the hell" manner that really expressed how we all felt about the situation.

"Shove the helm over," I directed William. "Head her up."

He obeyed, but still the boat refused to respond. I made another and larger sea anchor and launched it over the bow. It was useless. The cutter lay in the trough of the waves, as though nothing would induce her to fight them head on. While we watched the bow, hoping for a sudden miraculous change of heart in the cutter, a huge roller broke beside the cockpit and in another instant the cabin and cockpit were flooded with water.

"Hang on to that helm!" I bellowed to William, who had let it go when the sea washed over him. "Keep trying to get her head up."

I lashed at the ropes which held the sea anchors, realizing that they were partly the cause of the accident. Once they were free, I dashed for the companionway and plunged up to my waist in the flooded cabin. The handpump was useless now and I grabbed a big pan. With Dirk to help me, we worked like madmen; I filling the pan and handing it up to Dirk who tossed the water overboard. For two hours we worked, never pausing an instant to catch our breath. If a second roller had washed over us before we had finished, it would have been all over. The boat couldn't have stood another flood and we would have gone down like a sodden bathtub.

Even without another roller, things couldn't have been much worse. Everything inside the cabin was soaked, half our rice was ruined, all our personal possessions and even the instruments waterlogged. It was a disheartening sight that we looked upon, once we got the water out of the cabin. We had to throw away the spoiled rice and do what we could to restore some semblance of order below. But we couldn't do much with the boat pitching as it was and we left the cabin in a sorry mess.

William was waging a losing fight with the helm, for he couldn't keep the bow headed into the wind more than a few seconds at a time. Once he'd get it set, the wind would shove us around again and we'd lie abeam of the waves at the mercy of every comber that came our way. The rain continued, adding its bit to the spray which kept the cockpit half awash. Only by using the handpump every ten minutes or so were we able to keep it from flooding.

I saw that the most important thing right now was to rig up some kind of makeshift sail, so we could get some response out of the helm. A blanket tied to the stub of the mast and held in place with odds and ends of rope did the trick. The wind was so strong that a handkerchief would have helped, and the blanket did its duty admirably. The helmsman was able to keep the bow headed into the wind and we were even conscious that we were getting some speed out of the boat.

We took one-hour watches that night, but the two who were supposed to be resting in the cabin had a nightmare existence. All the blankets were wet and our clothes in the same sodden mess. No one got any sleep. Lying in a sea-soaked cabin with our sorry predicament to contemplate and the driving rain to act as a lullaby wasn't exactly soothing. I preferred to spend most of the time in the cockpit and it was lucky I did, as someone had to be on hand to man the pump.

The following morning dawned—though we didn't see anything that looked like dawn on the gray horizon—and we had much the same dreary prospect before us as we'd had the previous day. I'd cut down the mast and made some headway with the new sail, but that was about all. The swells were greater than ever; huge combers five or six meters high with mighty curling crests came rushing down on us, each one looking as though it had but one purpose—to swamp our boat. I rigged a higher sternboard out of canvas and part of an old beer case to help keep some of the water out of the cockpit. It worked after a fashion, though the spray made it necessary to pump every twenty minutes or so.

The storm lasted four days; days of gray skies, frequent soaking rain squalls, and a constant leaden dampness in the air which held our spirits down to zero. The wind kept up, though it veered slowly from southeast to north, while we were pushed along in its path by our blanket sail. It was hard to work in the wind and rain, particularly with the tools we had at hand. But we finished splicing the stays and cut a mainsail to fit the new mast. Now we would have to wait for the storm to die down before trying to hoist the mast into position. I wondered how we were going to get that unwieldy length of wood on our shoulders in that pitching boat, in order to set it up. But there was no use worrying about that until I had to.

Not once during those four days were we able to cook a meal. We lived on chocolate, a diet that was nourishing enough, but scarcely sufficient for anyone who was living and working as we were then. None of us had time for any philosophic consideration of our position or our chances of getting out of the mess alive. When there's an immediate task to be done, you don't have a chance to think. I don't remember having a thought in my head, except in connection with the work at hand; either sewing sail, splicing rope, or handling the helm. We were too busy even to worry. Of course we groused a lot, but that's a healthy sign and the more Dirk and William sweated and stewed the better I liked it. I don't believe any one us slept more than a total of three or four hours during those hellish four days, and we felt groggy with weariness.

On the morning of the eighteenth, it stopped raining and at about eleven o'clock a watery sunlight showed through the clouds. The mast was ready to be set up and the sails cut, so I decided to make the attempt that day. The cutter was still pitching heavily, but we couldn't afford to wait much longer for better weather. It was no use, however. The mast was too heavy for us to lift on our shoulders on that unstable footing and after two hours of cursing and sweating we had to give it up.

"Now what?" The question came from Dirk and from its tone I knew that he had about reached the depths of despair.

"I'll cut another hunk off it," I said, trying to act as though this were going to be an easy job. I didn't say that with a shorter mast, I'd have to recut the mainsail again. No use telling him all the bad news at once.

I got to work with the breadknife, deciding to take another four feet off which would leave us with a mast about twelve feet long. I felt sure we could get one of that length on our shoulders and set it up. The boat rolled as much as it ever had, making my work on deck a precarious job. I braced myself with one arm about the mast stump and began the slow process of whittling at the wood, a sliver at a time.

The sun disappeared an hour after its half-hearted appearance, and shortly after noon a heavy rain began to fall, one that seemed to have every intention of keeping on forever. I looked up from my work and saw Dirk handing one of the revolvers to William.

"What the hell are you doing with that?" I shouted.

Dirk clutched at the edge of the lurching boat and said grimly, "If we don't get out of this and it doesn't look as though we were, I'd rather die by a bullet than by drowning."

I didn't answer him. I was beginning to feel pretty much the same way myself.

CHAPTER EIGHTEEN

BUT the next morning I forgot all about putting a bullet through my head. I'd finished cutting down the mast and the rain stopped. The sun couldn't get through the heavy curtain of clouds hanging just over our heads, but the whole outlook began to seem brighter. I doled out the last three chocolate bars for breakfast and looked at the finished mast with some complacency.

"We'll get it up all right," I said confidently. "Come on, you two, let's get going."

Perhaps encouraged by my certainty, William and Dirk set their shoulders to the job with a will. Even to my surprise, we got the mast upright on the first try, a pretty amazing job considering the fact that we had to work with one hand and hang on to the boat with the other. The butt end fitted into the hinge as though it were tailored for it. Half an hour later, we all sat back in the cockpit and stared up at that twelve-foot length of wood rising over our heads as though it were Jack's beanstalk grown there overnight. To us it was just as miraculous as that. It meant the difference between safety and wreck, life and death.

"I better give that hinge another turn with the screwdriver," I said, after several minutes' silent enjoyment of the spectacle. "Want to be sure it's tight."

I stepped forward feeling suddenly so sure of myself and my own powers that I ignored the heave and roll of the boat entirely, trying to balance myself on my feet alone. My carelessness almost proved my finish. I had just reached the foot of the mast when a wave slapped the side of the boat with a sound like a cannon shot. The cutter gave a lurch and a second later I was overboard, several feet below the surface, blinded by the impact of the water.

When I fought my way up to the air, I found myself staring into the horrified faces of William and Dirk, who had rushed to the side to help me. But their willing hands stretched toward me weren't necessary. I'd surfaced just beside the stern and a moment later had hauled myself back into the boat, a soggier and wiser man.

"Good God, what happened?" cried Dirk, still staring at me as though I had risen out of the waves like the old man of the sea.

"What's the matter? Scared?" I asked, grinning at his terror-stricken face. "Thought you'd lost your navigator?"

"Yeah, well, what would have happened if you'd pegged out?" he demanded. "William and I would have been in one hell of a fix."

"So would I," I replied. "I'd be dead. All you two would have to do is sail west. You couldn't miss hitting the coast of Africa."

But the idea of sailing the cutter without my help didn't seem to amuse them very much and they kept a wary eye on me from then on. Every time I went forward they'd watch me like a couple of mother hens, and I began to wonder whether they were more worried about me as a navigator or a friend.

As though to celebrate our getting the mast up, the sun broke through the clouds shortly after noon, and I got a chance to take a sight, before it ducked behind the mist again. Our position showed Latitude 10 41 45 S, Longitude 92 28 45 E, which meant that we had covered more than three hundred miles since July fourteenth, averaging about sixty miles a day. Not bad considering we were using a blanket for a sail, and we had been going in the right direction all the time, too. It proved the strength of the wind and, in spite of the headaches that wind had given us in the past few days, we all felt grateful to it now we knew what it had done for us.

That afternoon I cut a jib from some of our spare canvas, a patchwork job that looked like a bedsheet on a pole, but it worked. I rigged it to help us get the most out of the wind, while I began the tedious process of recutting the mainsail for the second time. The wind still kept up a good fresh blow, but now with the jib to help us, it was easier for the helmsman to keep her headed up. The boat rocked less, but still enough to make us wonder what it would be like not to feel as though we were living in a washing machine. The rain came on again that afternoon, but it had lost much of its power to dampen us. Everything aboard, including ourselves, was so waterlogged that a little more rain only meant an extra few minutes at the pump.

Feeling that we needed something to warm us up on the inside at least, we cooked some rice that evening, a precarious business with the stove slithering around the cockpit and hot coals flying out in all directions. But we got some rice half cooked and all felt a lot better for the center of warmth it created where it would do the most good.

The next morning the wind veered around to north northwest, which sent us along toward the southeast in the wrong direction. We hadn't sail enough to tack and we had to sit by and watch ourselves being shoved off our course at a good rate of five or six knots. But the wind sent the clouds flying before it and just before noon the sun came out in the first real blaze of heat we had felt for days. We rushed everything on deck—blankets, clothes, and canvas—to dry in the blessed warmth. The heat felt like a benediction on our backs and with the dry wind to help we were soon dried out.

I got another sight that day that showed we had made seventy-five miles since the previous noon—seventy-five miles in the wrong direction, however. But I couldn't worry about that. I knew we'd hit the southeast trades as soon as the last tag ends of the storm had blown away. It was enough to be thankful we'd come through that hell alive, without complaining about an adverse wind. I got to work on the mainsail and showed William and Dirk how to sew canvas. By the next morning, July twenty-first, we had it finished, the weirdest sail ever seen on any ocean. It was a long, awkward, triangular affair that would make an honest seaman blink, but it had the outstanding virtue of working. No matter how it looked, once I got it rigged it did its duty like a gentleman.

We spent the afternoon trying to get the boat in some kind of order; cleaning out the cabin, clearing the deck, and in general drying out and stowing away our stuff. I wanted to have everything ready when we hit the trade wind, so we could give all our attention to sailing the boat and not bother with housekeeping.

William had rigged a fishing line over the stern and just before it was time to eat that evening, we saw a big fish bobbing along behind us, caught fast on the hook. We hauled it in, considerably cheered by the thought of variety in our monotonous diet. It was a benito, a big fellow with an ugly face, but plump enough to make us think we'd get a good meal out of him. William sat up in the bow to clean him, while Dirk got some water boiling on the stove. The wind was still blowing at a good stiff rate, but with our makeshift sails we were able to keep the bow headed into the waves and so did not pitch quite as much. The stove stayed more or less stationary and we had gotten into our cooking routine again.

The benito tasted fine and I ate about as much as I could hold. But I didn't hold it long. Either it wasn't cooked enough or I have too ladylike a stomach. I spent a miserable night, not at all helped by William and Dirk, who pretended to think I was seasick and got back at me for teasing them about their *mal de mer* by giving me an unmerciful ribbing. I recovered by morning, however, but I let the other two finish what was left of the fish. Rice and corned beef looked all right to me.

The morning of the twenty-second showed a bright sky filled with scudding clouds, the last of the storm signals. The wind was still from the northwest, but it was dropping and I felt sure we'd hit the trades again some time that day. The noon sight showed we had covered another sixty miles in the wrong direction. It was beginning to get pretty cold and I hoped we wouldn't be forced much farther south of the equator. We weren't prepared for antarctic weather by any means and the previous night had given us a taste of what Admiral Byrd went through. Even with dry blankets again, we'd all felt pretty chilly.

In the evening we hit them, the welcome southeast trade winds. They blew on us like a benediction, sending us west on our course toward Rodriguez, some 1600 miles away. We'd covered almost half the voyage, lived through a storm and near wreck and now were on our way once more. We began to enjoy life. The routine of life aboard a small boat began again as though it had never been interrupted. We organized our watches on the old schedule, got a full quota of sleep, and ate a morning and evening meal.

William and Dirk had begun to get the feel of the helm and now I didn't have to worry so much when they were on watch. All shifting of sail was up to me, however, and I was kept too busy to have time for any idle contemplation of the "boundless sea" that the poets like to think about. As I've said before, I don't believe I thought about anything beyond the deck of that cutter the whole time I was at sea. There is always something to be done on a small ship and I, as skipper, had my hands full. We spent more time talking, though; making plans for what we should do when we hit Rodriguez and speculating on our reception by the British there. We knew they'd probably confiscate our boat and wait for instructions from the Netherlands government before letting us go on. All of us had but one idea in mind; to join the Netherlands Army and fight the Japs. It didn't matter to us what happened as long as we were allowed to do that.

Three days later on July twenty-fifth we'd covered 315 miles, all of them toward Rodriguez. An average run of a hundred miles a day wasn't bad, considering the state of our sails. They'd begun to give me a lot of trouble; the canvas was old and my sailmaking with darning needles and cord was of necessity a patchwork job. I spent most of the time during those three days mending the tears and worn spots, hoping the threadbare canvas would hold out until we reached our goal.

But I was out of luck as far as the sails were concerned. Another three days of wind, which averaged us the same hundred miles per day, was too much for them. I had to begin work on another set of sails. It was now the twenty-eighth of July and we'd been at sea three weeks, most of the time with nothing to look at but an endless expanse of heaving sea, a bowl-like sky overhead, and the narrow confines of the cutter near at hand. The nights were getting colder, but now our thin tropical blood was getting used to them and the bracing air really made us feel a lot better. We were all tanned to a mahogany brown and fit as the proverbial fiddles. The trip, except for the four days of storm and near disaster, was turning out to be quite a pleasure voyage.

I didn't mind the work I had to do on the new sails, as it gave me something to relieve the monotony of the long days. William and Dirk weren't as fortunate, for, except for their turns at the helm, they had nothing to do, but wish for a change of scene. As I look back on it, it's a wonder none of us got into a quarrel. Three men cooped up on a twenty-five-foot cutter with nothing but each other's faces to look at are apt to get a little touchy. But we were all keyed up by the immensity of our adventure and the knowledge that, if we succeeded in it, we would have a real job to do—fighting Japs. All of us are pretty easy-going anyway, not given to "nerves" or petty bickering, and we got along with very few harsh words. As skipper I had the authority to step on any incipient quarrels, and, as soon as I saw one brewing among us, I shut it up in a hurry. The only thing that "got" us was the dreary sameness of our food and the scarcity of water. But there was no one to blame this on and it didn't cause any more trouble than a good deal of vehement grousing.

"Let's open another can of fruit," suggested Dirk on the evening of the twenty-ninth. "You say we just passed the eightieth meridian, so let's celebrate it."

"Suits me," I replied, willing to find any cause for celebration. "What I'll really feel glad about is the day I take the last stitch in these lousy sails."

"How are they coming?" asked William, who was at the helm. "I should— Hey!"

His exclamation made us all start and we looked up to see him pointing toward the setting sun as though he had sighted land at the very least. It was a rainbow or rather a pair of them, fitting into each other in two perfectly semi-circular curves, brilliant and clearly outlined against the western sky. None of us said anything, but we all took the rainbows as good omens. They arched just over the spot toward which we were headed and seemed to form a gateway on our course. We were enormously cheered by the sight, and even the drenching rain squall which followed as the rainbows disappeared could not quench our good spirits.

But during the night the rain increased and with it the wind. By morning the mainsail was in ribbons, much too far gone for repair. We got it down and sailed the rest of the day with the jib alone, while I redoubled my efforts to finish the new sail. It was ready that evening and hoisted after a tough hour's work. William and Dirk had never had to rig a new sail before, but it was blowing too hard for me to do it alone, so I had to enlist their services. The new sail looked worse than the one I'd made before, but like its predecessor, it worked, sending us along at a good six knots.

The wind increased during the night and by the morning of August first it was blowing so hard that a long rip showed along the bottom of the sail. I knew the canvas was none too strong, but I'd hoped it would stand up better than this.

"Have to take her in to mend that tear," I said resignedly. Another gust of rain hit us just then and considerably dampened my already low-pressure enthusiasm for the job.

"Why don't you let it alone?" asked Dirk. "It might not get any bigger."

I didn't even answer him and began to haul in the sail. I did a patch job of mending it, for the wind was hitting us too hard to try to take the whole thing down again right now. We were now about six hundred miles due west of Rodriguez and at the rate we were going should reach the island in four or five days. I wasn't going to get careless when we were so near our goal.

The rain stopped by noon and I got a sight that showed we were Latitude 18 41 05 S, Longitude 74 12 15 E, a run of 136 miles since the previous day. We were really hitting it up now with a good strong wind that would have sent us along at a couple of knots even without sails. It turned out to be a beautiful sunny day, warm and clear, a good start, we all thought, for the new month. William began to make a Dutch flag out of an old red hockey stocking, a white shirt, and a blue sport jacket.

"Want to let them know who we are when we reach Rodriguez," he explained, when I asked him what he was doing.

"They'll find out who we are soon enough," I told him.

"We won't need a flag, but, if you want to make one, go ahead."

I was glad he'd found something to occupy himself with, though I knew a Dutch flag wasn't necessary. When we reached Rodriguez we'd have no trouble identifying ourselves, and it wasn't likely that the British there would fire on a small boat before they knew who we were.

I spent the next three days nursing that mainsail. The patched tear didn't hold, and on the night of the third the sail ripped from end to end along the bottom. We had to take it in, just as a rain squall struck us, giving us a good freezing chill to make the work all the harder. Without lights we had a rough time on the heeling deck and it took us a good half hour to get it down.

Sailing under the jib alone the next day cut our speed down to about two knots. But we were within three hundred and fifty miles of Rodriguez now and we didn't let this worry us. I cut the bottom off the mainsail, which shortened it considerably and made it look worse than ever, which isn't saying much for it. We got it up the next morning and the noon sight showed we'd made ninety-two miles, just on the jib. It seemed as though nothing could stop us and we were all in high spirits. Now that we were getting so near Rodriguez, food rationing wasn't necessary and we cooked ourselves two whopping big meals that day.

"I'll never look a plate of rice in the face again," vowed Dirk that evening. "As for corned beef—" He didn't finish, but sat looking at the unappetizing mess on his plate with an expression that said more than words.

"You'll be eating white bread in Rodriguez the day after tomorrow," I told him confidently.

Both William and Dirk looked at me in utter disbelief. They either couldn't believe the good news or thought I was talking through my hat. All around us was the same gray expanse of sea, the same sky and water we had looked at for four long weeks. The idea that we would actually reach Rodriguez in two days was too much for them to comprehend.

"Want to bet?" I asked.

CHAPTER NINETEEN

IT'S lucky neither William nor Dirk took me up on that bet. Lucky for them, that is. At noon on August fifth our position was Latitude 19 34 10 S, Longitude 65 56 30 E, showing a run of ninety-two miles since the previous day. According to my rough calculations, we were some one hundred and forty miles east of Rodriguez. I hoped that's where we were at least. That publicity map of the Indian Ocean wasn't good enough to base an exact judgment on. I knew that Rodriguez was a small island; on my map it was about one-tenth of an inch long. If we could hit that pin dot in the expanse of the ocean, we'd be more than fortunate, we'd be pretty darn good.

"What's the name of the town on Rodriguez?" asked William that evening. "I'd like to know where it is I'm to eat this white bread."

"Port Mathurin," I answered, staring at the map. "It shows here on the east side of the island, which seems pretty funny to me. It can't be much of a harbor. The swell from the ocean, sweeping all across from Australia, must make it a lousy anchorage."

"You can't tell anything from that map," said Dirk scornfully. "Rodriguez is so small there, you'd never know where Port Mathurin is. Which side are you going to approach it from? How do you know where the reefs are?"

"I don't," I answered. "We'll just have to trust to luck."

"It'll be luck if we hit it at all," said Dirk, who still couldn't believe that land lay ahead on that barren expanse of sea. "I'll believe it when I see it."

I didn't sleep that night. I couldn't. I knew that at the rate we were going we ought to sight Rodriguez early the next morning, if my calculations were right. The nearer we came to that dot on the ocean, the bigger that "if" looked to me. I was at the helm the next morning, taking the six o'clock watch while William and Dirk were below, trying to catch some sleep. We'd been making about six knots all night and a heavy swell showed the strength of the wind. The cutter climbed laboriously up those mountains of water and slid thankfully down into the troughs on the other side.

At eight o'clock the boat reached the crest of one of those watery hills and just before it dipped down the opposite slope, I saw it. Dead ahead, showing faintly gray in the morning light, lay the island of Rodriguez. For a moment I didn't say anything. If I'd wanted to shout the time-honored "land ho" I wouldn't have been able to. My throat felt thick. I waited until the cutter mounted the next swell, just to make certain that my eyes hadn't deceived me. They hadn't. There it was, already clearer, more distinct in the bright morning sun. We'd done it. Then I yelled.

"We hit it!" I bellowed in a voice that would have waked the dead. It roused William and Dirk, who came clattering up on deck in ten seconds flat.

"Where?" asked Dirk accusingly, peering ahead at the steep rise of water towering before us. "You're joking."

"Like hell I am," I answered joyfully. "Wait until we hit the top of this swell and— There! Look at it!" I pointed toward the now clearly defined spot of land directly before us.

"Well I'll be damned," said William softly.

Dirk didn't say anything. He stared ahead of him, as though still unable to believe his eyes.

They couldn't doubt it a few minutes later. Each heave of the little cutter, breasting the tops of the swells, brought us that much nearer. Soon we could make out the shape of the rocky hills which covered the island, making it a jagged mass of irregular outlines.

"Which side of it are you going to tackle?" asked William, later in the morning. "When do you think we'll get there?"

"Oh, around one or two o'clock," I replied. "Those breakers on this end don't look too good to me. Guess I'll try the north side."

"Why?" It was Dirk who asked the question.

I shrugged. "I don't know. Just a hunch. It's obvious the map was wrong about Port Mathurin. It's not at this end."

We could see the island clearly now; the steep hills and the long stretches of green pasture, dotted with grazing cows. It seemed almost unbelievable to be looking at that peaceful scene, after our long days at sea. None of us talked much; we just feasted our eyes on the greenery and in imagination felt our feet touching dry land once more.

At two in the afternoon we were within half a mile of the shore, just off the southeast corner of the island. There was a heavy cloud of breakers dashing against the coast, sending up a high spray that soaked the steep rocks which covered the shoreline. Obviously there was no hope of finding an anchorage here. I tacked northward for a mile or so and then headed west along the north coast. Here, too, there was no sign of a safe harbor. The same breakers betrayed the reefs about the island, dangerous waters for us. I stayed as close to land as possible without getting caught in the ground swell and wondered if I'd guessed wrong in choosing this side of the island to find a landing place.

"Hey, look at those people on the hill there," cried Dirk, pointing to a wide pasture land, a picturesque scene of grazing cows and men and women dressed in bright-colored clothes. "They seem to be watching us."

"Probably are," I answered. "It isn't every day a sailing boat flying a Dutch flag lands here, you can bet."

We waved at the watchers, but either they didn't see us or were too astounded at our appearance to be able to reply. The sails we carried must have made them think we were guests from another planet anyway. No boat had ever carried worse-looking canvas than we did, of that I'm certain. I kept my eyes on the mainsail, praying that it would hold out for another hour or so. If it had given way again just then, it might have been all up with us. The wind would have carried us straight for the breakers, where we'd have been ground to pieces; not a pretty end to a voyage like ours.

At the northwest corner of the island I sighted a long reef stretching out into the ocean for half a mile. I had to veer north to avoid this and by the time we had cleared it and were headed toward the island once more, we could make out the houses and radio masts in the town of Port Mathurin. I had been right in my doubt of the map after all; Port Mathurin was on the west end of the island, just where I suspected it was. Then I spotted another reef stretching westward all across the water which separated us from the town.

I began to swear half to myself. If we had to sail out around that long reef, the end of which I couldn't see from where we were, it would be nightfall before we could drop anchor. Then I saw a pair of stakes, marking a passage through the reef. It was the entrance to the harbor of Port Mathurin.

We ran through the narrow cut, guided by the changed color of the water in the channel. Once in the little bay the wind slackened and we coasted slowly toward the town, now lying before us in the bright afternoon sun. About four hundred yards off shore I lowered sail, for I could see that the water was growing shallower with every foot. The little cutter drifted easily and lazily forward, as though weary from its long fight against the sea. Slowly and surely she nosed forward, then stopped. We had run aground.

I looked up. Coming toward us was a small power boat. At its bow was a British flag, snapping briskly in the wind. I turned to William and Dirk.

"Well," I said inadequately, "we made it."

A major of the British forces stationed on the island took us in charge; a very astonished major, who had to be told over and over again the story of our trip. He brought us ashore, fed us, gave us a place to sleep and confiscated our boat. We didn't care about that. The long trip was over, our adventure had succeeded. We were free to fight again.

The week we spent on Rodriguez passed pleasantly. The British Army forces treated us well and promised to see that we got in touch with the Netherlands government. The islanders themselves were equally hospitable; they couldn't make enough of us and we were deluged with kindness and questions. None of them ever tired of hearing the story of our trip.

I found that the luck which had followed us for the past month hadn't deserted us when I happened to choose the north side of the island to find a possible harbor. From a hilltop I saw the long reefs stretching out to the south, the breakers pounding the shore. If I'd come in along the south coast with the wind as it was, we might never have made Port Mathurin.

A British cruiser picked us up on August eleventh with instructions from the Netherlands government to take us to Ceylon. That was the first leg of the long journey that brought me to America, sent Dirk to Australia, and William to England. In each one of these places we were to prepare ourselves for the job we'd set out to do—fighting Japs. We parted at Ceylon. I've seen neither of them since. But we will meet again—in Java. When we return, we will be the invaders, we and our Dutch comrades.

www.ingramcontent.com/pod-product-compliance
Lightning Source LLC
Chambersburg PA
CBHW071418150726
48000CB00001B/384